HOME FASHIONS

Curtains, Bedspreads, Valances, Swags, Pillows & Accessories

500 Colour Photographs

500 Decorating Ideas

M. Demir

HOME FASHIONS
Curtains, Bedspreads, Valances, Swags, Pillows & Accessories

Prepared by Mehmet Demir on behalf of Ankara Textile Industry and Trading Incorporated. All rights owned by Mehmet Demir on behalf of Ankara Textile Industry and Trading Incorporated.

D.P.C Publishing
Phone: +90-212-425-7888
Fax: +90-212-425-7889
Internet: www.homefashion.org
E-mail: info@homefashion.org

Printed in Turkey

USA, Canada and South America Distribution:
Randall International
1407 North Batavia St., Suite 201, Orange, CA 92867, USA
Phone: (714) 771-8488
Fax: (714) 771- 3958
Tollfree: (800) 882-8907 (US Only)
Internet: www.randallonline.com
E-mail: sales@randallonline.com

We would like to thank Taksim Park Plaza Hotel, Home Textile Association, Linda Jenkins, Caroline Mickey and Sevim Zor for their contributions.

Publisher
D.P.C. Publishing

Publishing Manager
Mehmet Demir

Publishing Coordinator
Bedriye Yavuz

Editor-in-Chief
Melanie Bysouth

Editors (Graphics and Design)
Yilmaz Kocer
Ebru Demir
R.O. Yavuz
Metin Kerimoglu

Director of Operations
Hasim Buyukbalci

Model Planning
Bedriye Yavuz
David Warchol
Paul Watson
Elizabeth Bright
Andrew Merrell
Svetlana Anoskina

Decorations
Alan Ryan
Alexander Kazantsev

Photographs
Bahadir Taskin
Selamet Taskin

Graphics
Ahmet Sevgi
Tarkan Sert

Text
Melanie Bysouth

Cover Design
Diego Linares

Contents

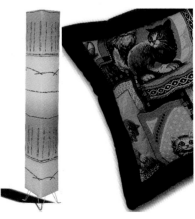

Preface...

One's home is often a reflection of who they are. From puddled velvet draperies wrapped with braided tiebacks to romantic sheer curtains gently swirled around a gilded rod, from a pink and white Kingston valance to a red and gold tear drop valance, from a tasseled Empire swag and cascade combination to a simple violet balloon shade, the possibilities of window design are endless. And when decorating, we must never forget that with each choice we make we are expressing a part of ourselves and a window treatment can quickly become a detailed indication of who we are.

It is our hope that Home Fashions will become a guide to discovering how you may best reflect yourself in your home. As you turn the pages of this book you will find ideas, both simple and dramatic, for incorporating draperies, shades, blinds, swags and cascades and valances into your home and we hope that each window treatment you create will be a spirited representation of your individuality.

M. Devier.

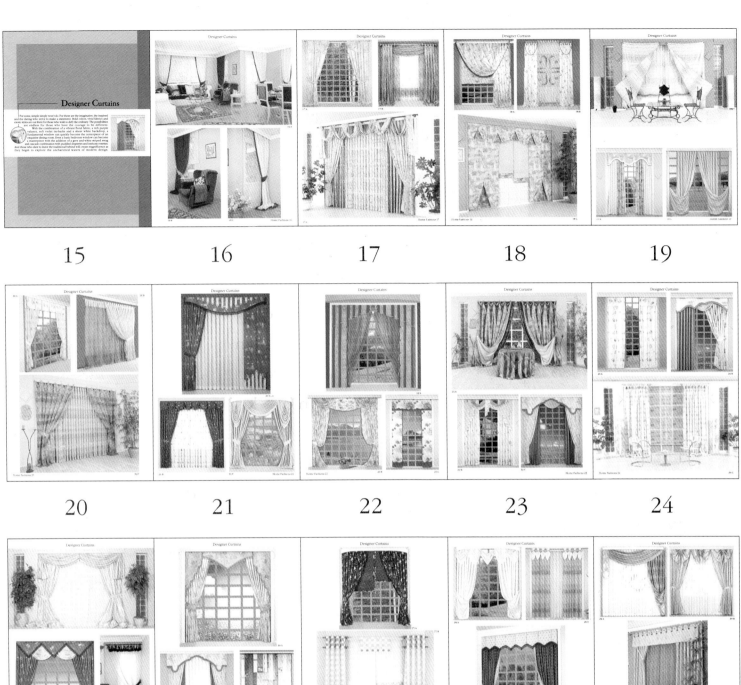

15

16

17

18

19

20

21

22

23

24

25

26

27

28

29

30

31

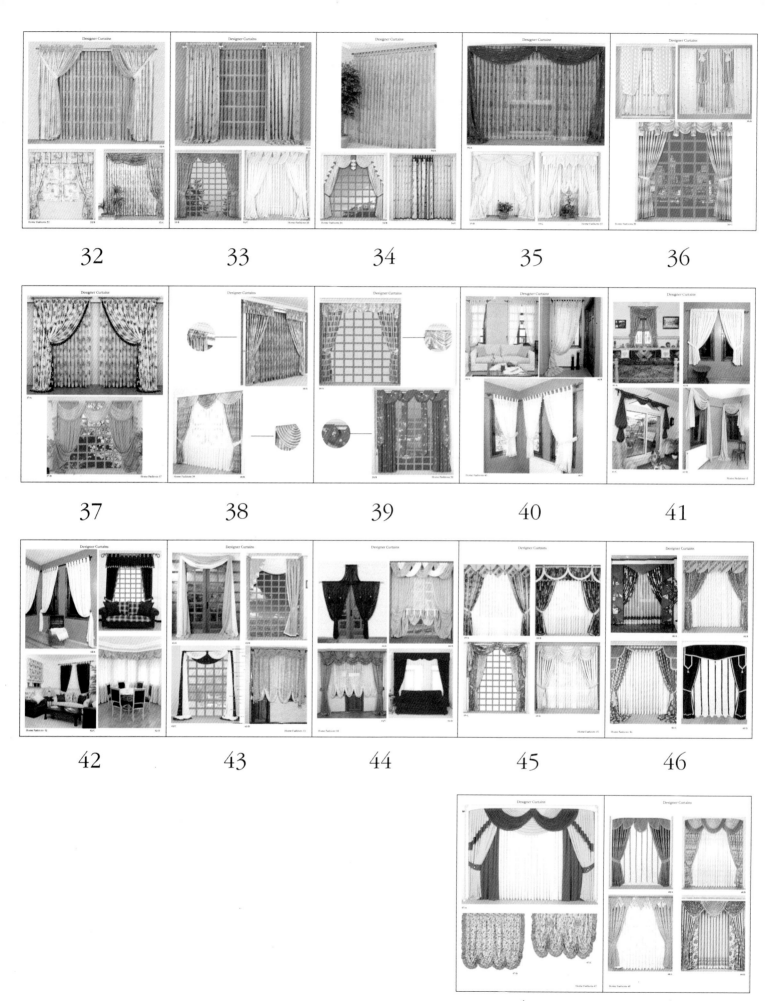

32

33

34

35

36

37

38

39

40

41

42

43

44

45

46

47

48

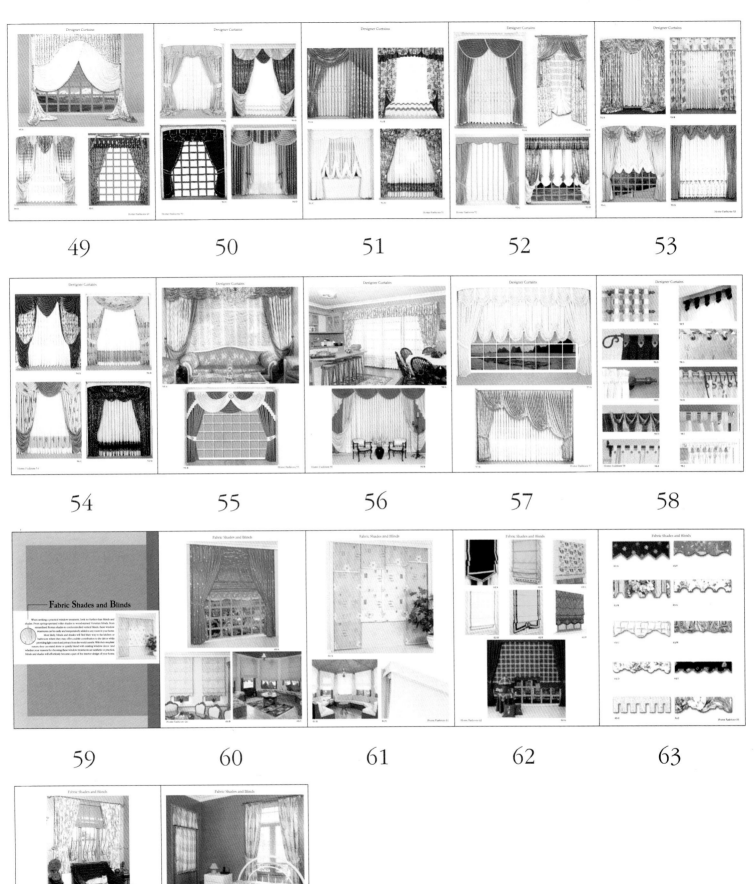

49

50

51

52

53

54

55

56

57

58

59

60

61

62

63

64

65

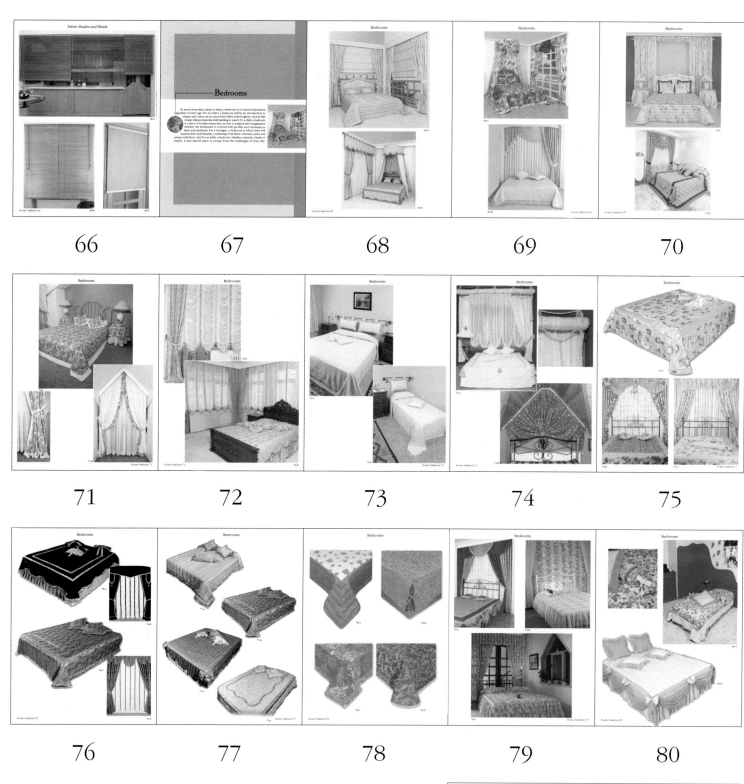

66

67

68

69

70

71

72

73

74

75

76

77

78

79

80

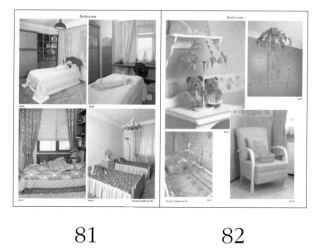

81

82

83

84

85

86

87

88

89

90

91

92

93

94

95

96

97

98

99

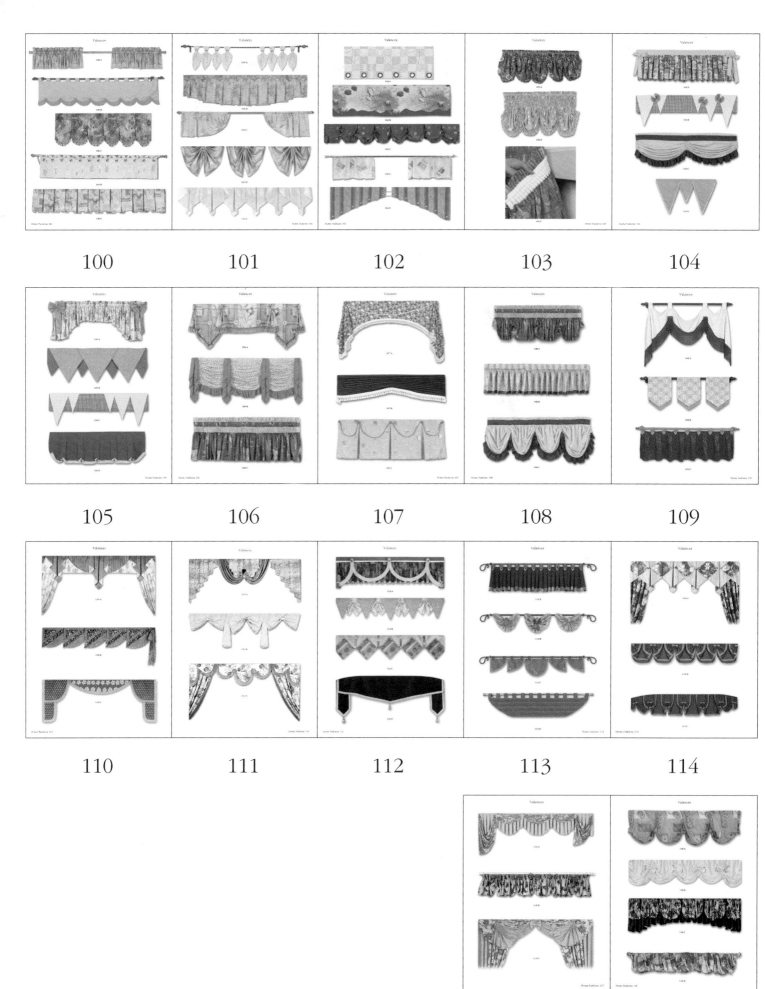

100

101

102

103

104

105

106

107

108

109

110

111

112

113

114

115

116

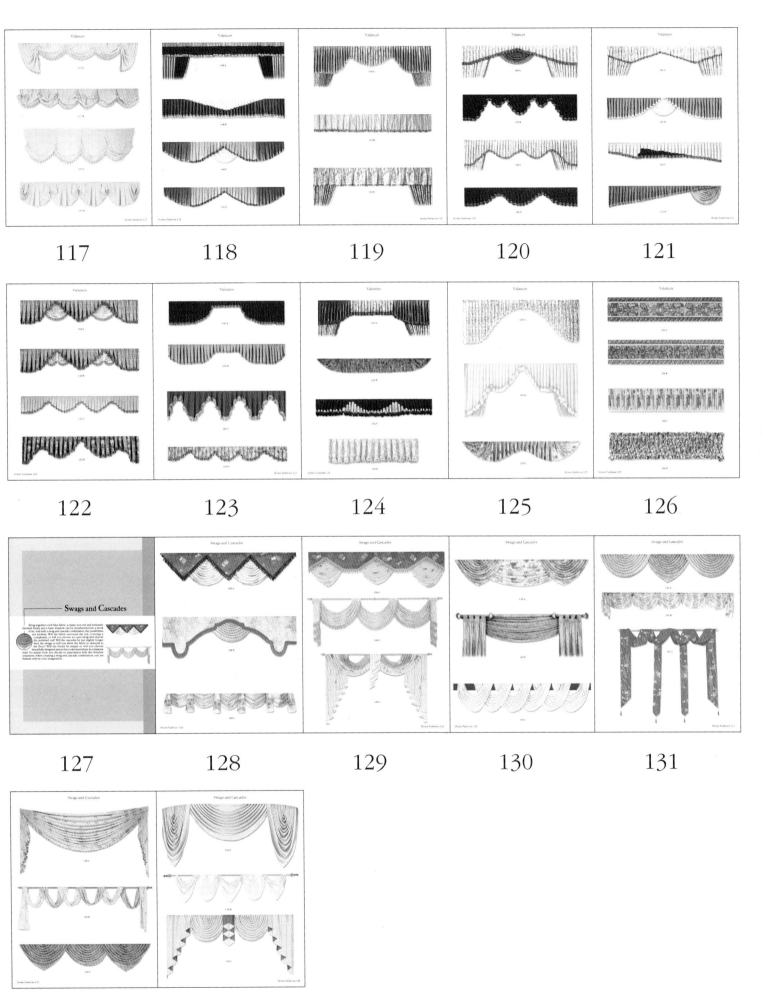

117

118

119

120

121

122

123

124

125

126

127

128

129

130

131

132

133

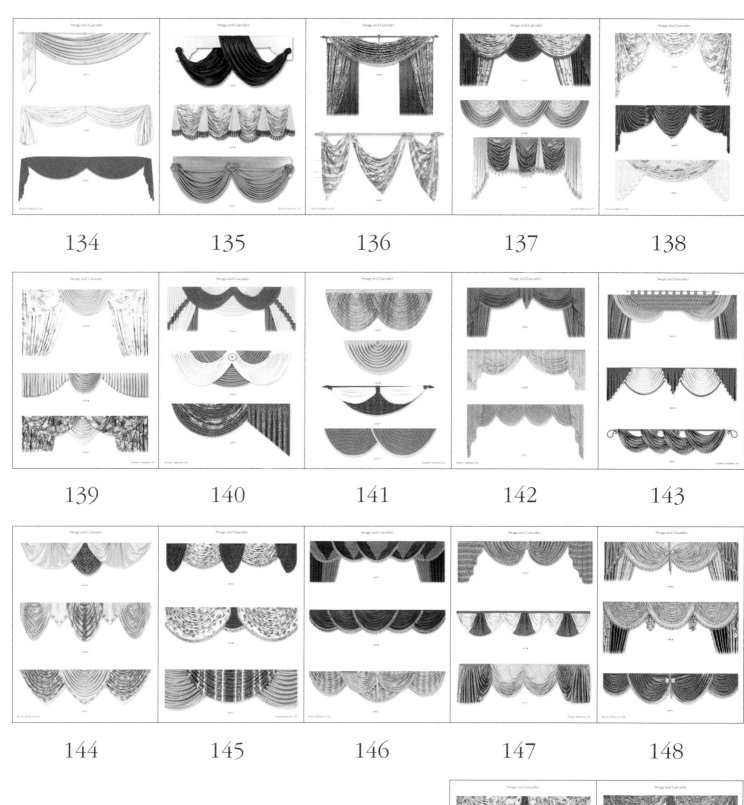

134

135

136

137

138

139

140

141

142

143

144

145

146

147

148

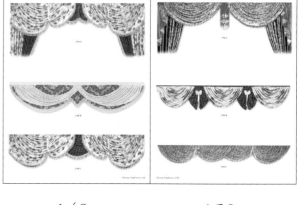

149

150

151

152

153

154

155

156

157

158

159

160

161

162

163

164

165

166

167

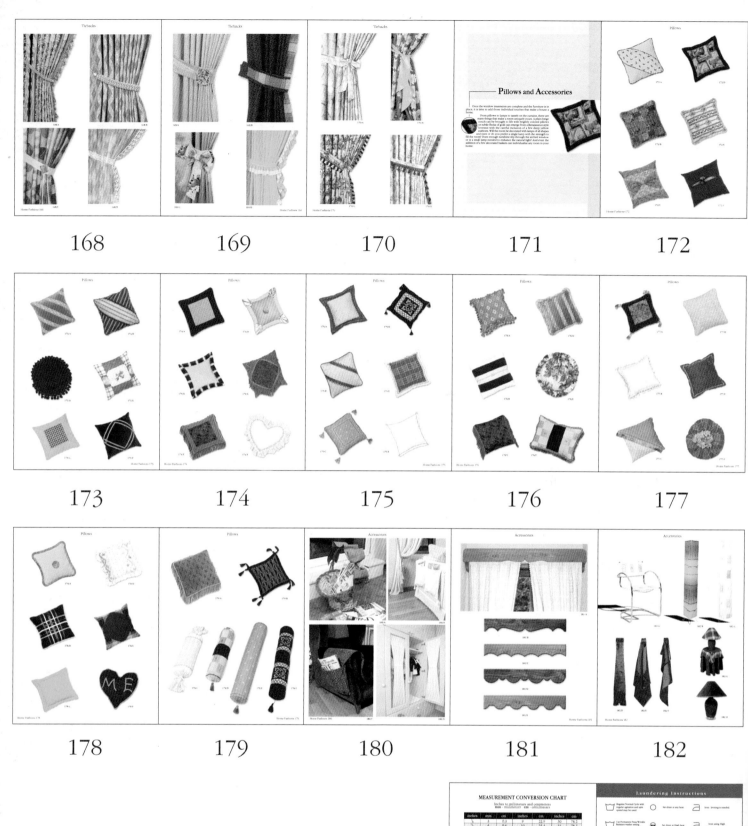

168

169

170

171

172

173

174

175

176

177

178

179

180

181

182

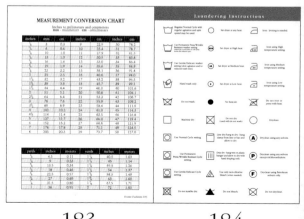

183

184

Designer Curtains

For some, simple simply won't do. For these are the imaginative, the inspired and the daring who strive to make a statement. Bold colors, vivid fabrics and exotic styles are out there for those who wish to defy the ordinary. The possibilities are endless for those who have the courage to be different. With the combination of a vibrant floral fabric, a rich purple valance, soft violet tie-backs and a sheer white backdrop, a fundamental window can quickly become the centerpiece of an exquisite dining room. Even a basic bedroom window can become a masterpiece with the addition of a grey and white striped swag and cascade combination with puddled draperies and intricate rosettes. And those who dare to leave the traditional behind will create magnificence as they begin to explore the unchartered waters of modern design.

Designer Curtains

Designer Curtains

17/A

17/B

17/C

18/A

18/B

18/C

19/A

19/B

19/C

Designer Curtains

Designer Curtains

21/A

21/B

21/C

22/A

22/B

22/C

Designer Curtains

23/A

23/B

23/C

Designer Curtains

24/A

24/B

24/C

25/A

25/B

·25/C

Designer Curtains

26/A

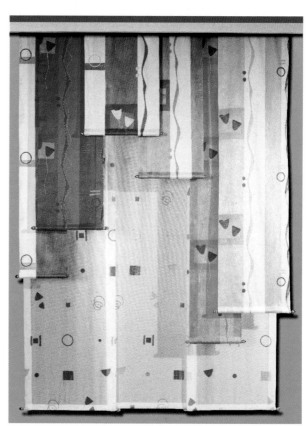

27/A

27/B

Designer Curtains

28/A

Designer Curtains

29/A

29/B

29/C

Designer Curtains

30/A

30/B

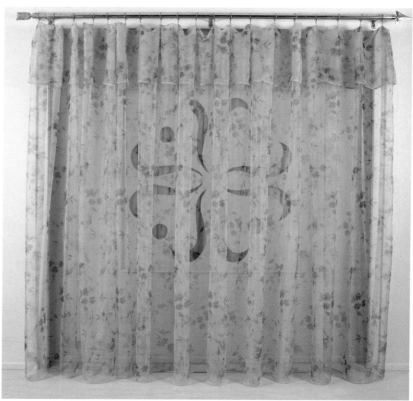

30/C

Designer Curtains

31/A

31/B

31/C

32/A

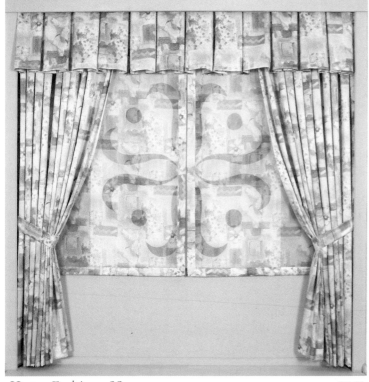

32/B

32/C

Designer Curtains

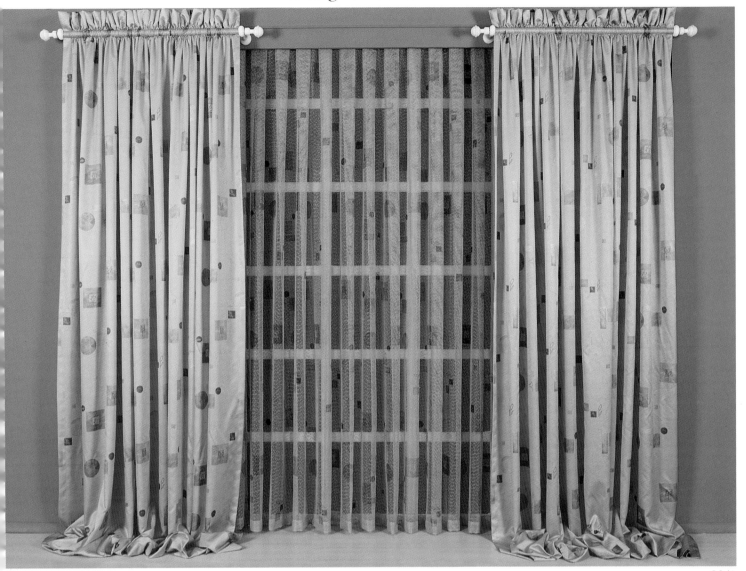

33/A

33/B

33/C

Home Fashions 33

Designer Curtains

34/A

34/B

34/C

Designer Curtains

35/A

35/B

35/C

Designer Curtains

36/A

36/B

36/C

37/A

37/B

Designer Curtains

38/A

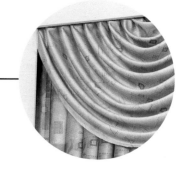

38/B

Designer Curtains

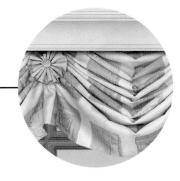

39/A

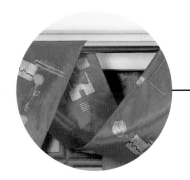

Designer Curtains

40/A

40/B

40/C

Designer Curtains

41/A

41/B

41/C

41/D

Designer Curtains

42/A

42/B

42/C

42/D

43/A

43/B

43/C

43/D

Designer Curtains

44/A

44/B

44/C

44/D

45/A

45/B

45/C

45/D

46/A

46/B

46/C

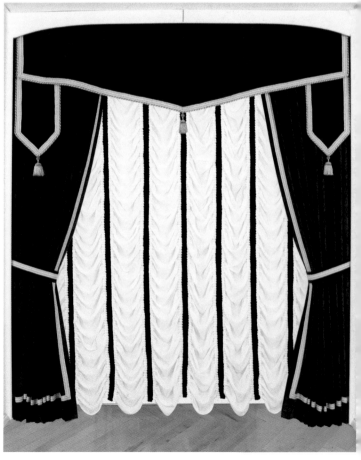

46/D

47/A

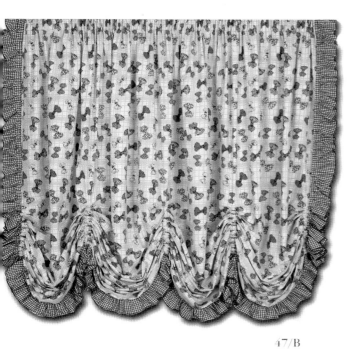

47/B

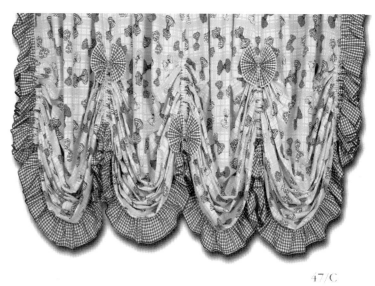

47/C

48/A

48/B

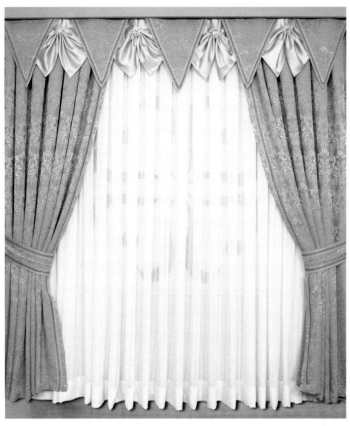

48/C

48/D

49/A

49/B

49/C

50/A

50/B

50/C

50/D

51/A

51/B

51/C

51/D

52/A

52/B

52/C

52/D

53/A

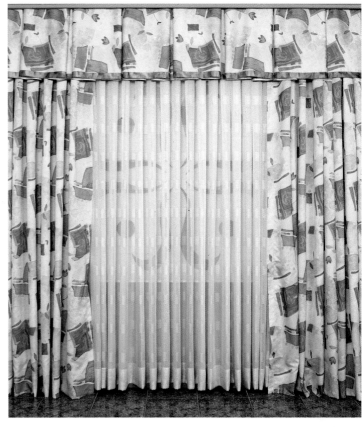

53/B

53/C

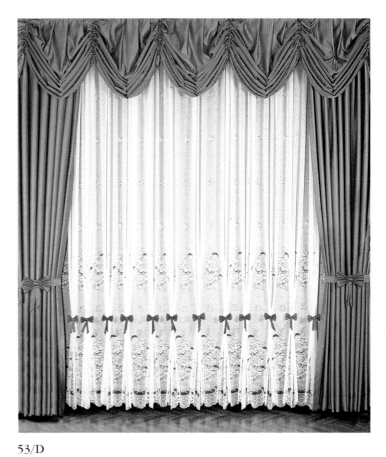

53/D

54/A

54/B

54/C

54/D

55/A

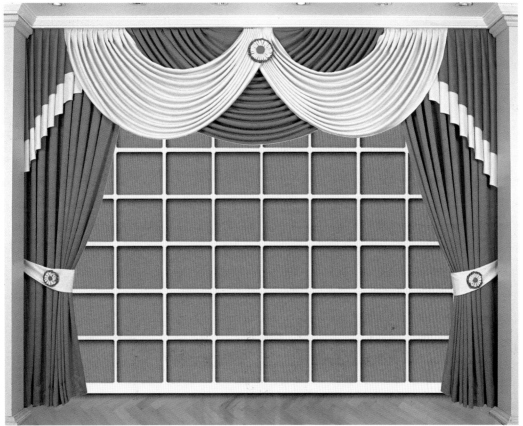

55/B

56/A

57/A

Designer Curtains

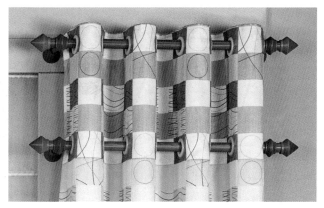

58/A

58/F

58/B

58/G

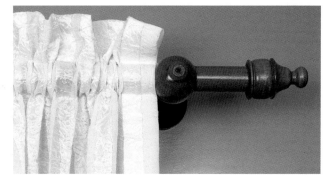

58/C

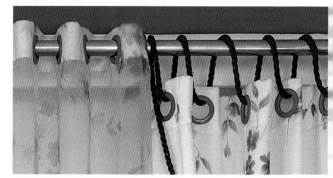

58/H

58/D

58/I

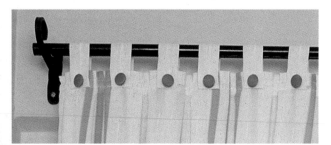

Home Fashions 58

58/E

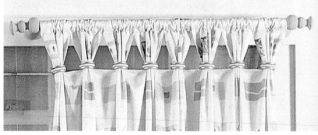

58/J

Fabric Shades and Blinds

When seeking a practical window treatment, look no further than blinds and shades. From spring-operated roller shades to wood-stained Venetian blinds, from streamlined Roman shades to cord-controlled vertical blinds, these window treatments can be easily and inexpensively added to any room in your home. Most likely, blinds and shades will find their way to the kitchen or bathroom where they may offer a subtle contribution to the décor while providing light control and privacy from the world outside. With their simplistic nature, they can stand alone or quietly blend with existing window decor. And whether your reasons for choosing these window treatments are aesthetic or practical, blinds and shades will effortlessly become a part of the interior design of your home.

Fabric Shades and Blinds

60/A

Fabric Shades and Blinds

61/A

61/B

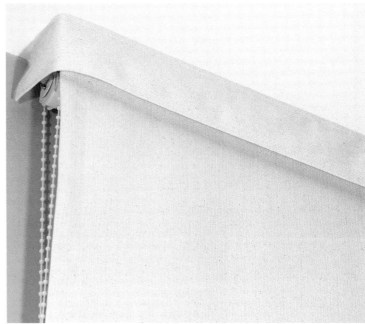

61/C

Fabric Shades and Blinds

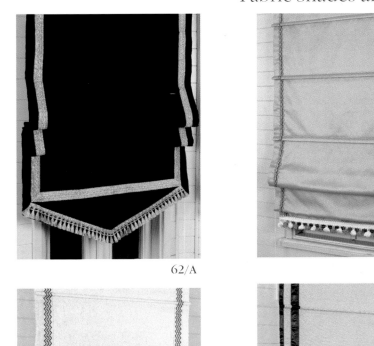

62/A

62/B

62/C

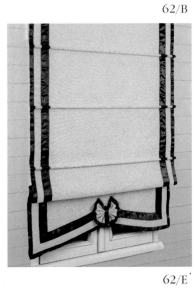

62/D

62/E´

62/F

62/G

Fabric Shades and Blinds

63/A

63/F

63/B

63/G

63/C

63/H

63/D

63/I

63/E

63/J

64/A

65/A

66/A

Bedrooms

So much more than a place to sleep, a bedroom is of utmost importance regardless of one's age. For an infant, a bedroom will be an introduction to shapes and colors, as an ocean blue fabric with brightly colored fish creates vibrant draperies with bedding to match. To a child, a bedroom is a place of wonder where they are free to explore their imagination whether the bedspread is covered with giraffes and elephants or ships and airplanes. For a teenager, a bedroom is where they will express their individuality, combining vivid fabric, dramatic paint and unique wall décor. And for an adult, a bedroom, whether romantic, classic or simple, is that special place to escape from the challenges of busy day.

68/A

68/B

69/A

69/B

70/A

70/B

71/A

71/B

71/C

72/A

73/A

73/B

74/A

74/B

75/A

75/B

75/C

76/A

76/B

76/C

76/D

77/A

77/B

77/C

77/D

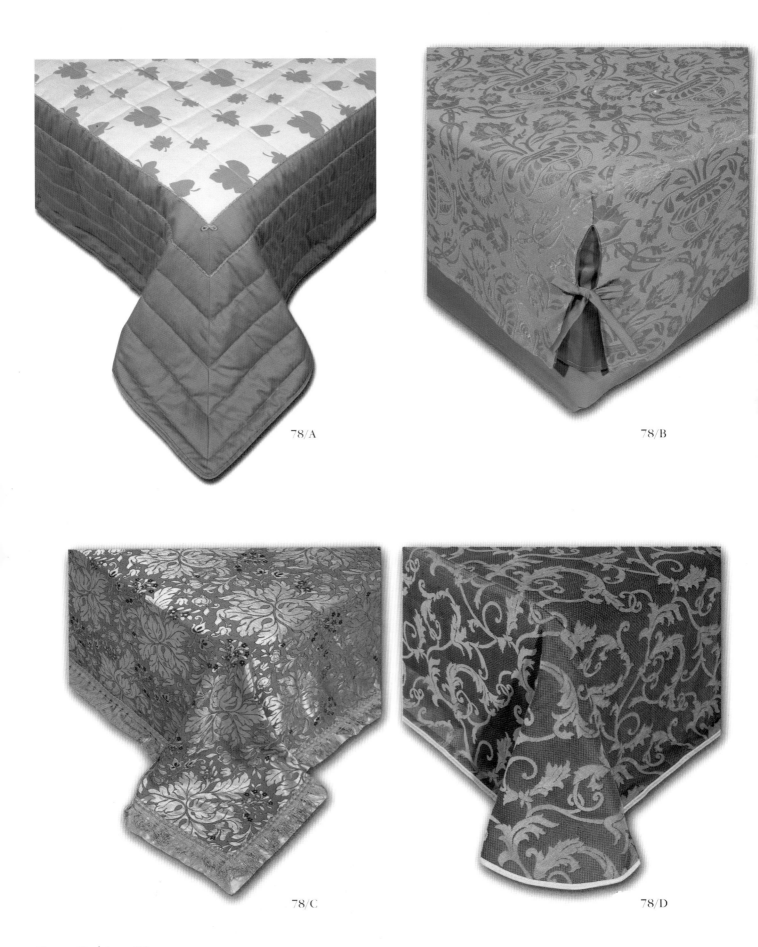

78/A

78/B

78/C

78/D

79/A

79/B

79/C

80/A

80/B

81/A

81/B

81/C

81/D

82/B

82/A

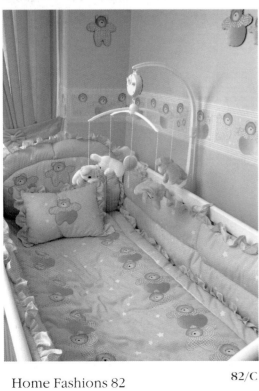

82/C

82/D

83/A

83/B

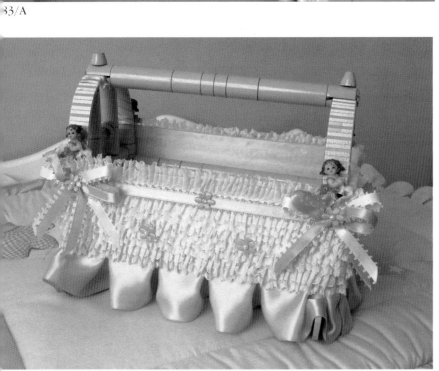

83/C

83/D

84/A

84/B

84/C

84/D

Hotel Rooms

It may not be the first thing you consider when selecting a hotel, but it will be the first thing you notice when you enter your room. Whether staying for a romantic getaway or a relaxing weekend with friends, the décor of a hotel room will not go unnoticed. From a country-style bed and breakfast to an Egyptian-themed Vegas casino, the look of the room cannot help but enhance your experience with the hotel. Beginning with window treatments and bedspreads, the theme of the room will grow to include striking lampshades, plush, comfortable chairs and detailed artwork. And while enjoying your stay, the design of the room may give you some new ideas to experiment with upon your return home.

Typically the room's centerpiece, bedding is perhaps the most important element to consider when decorating a 86/A
hotel room. A complete bed will consist of ten pieces, listed as follows:

01- Dust Ruffle

02- Dust Ruffle Cover

03- Mattress

04- Mattress Pad

05- Sheets

06- Quilt or Blanket

07- Quilt Cover

08- Pillows

09- Pillow Cases or Shams

10- Bedspread or Comforter

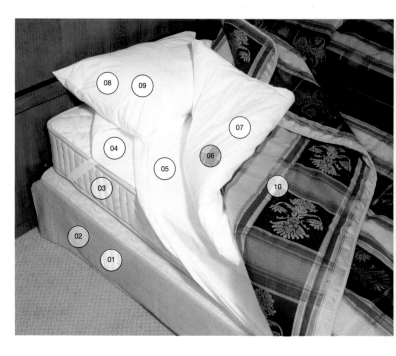

87/A

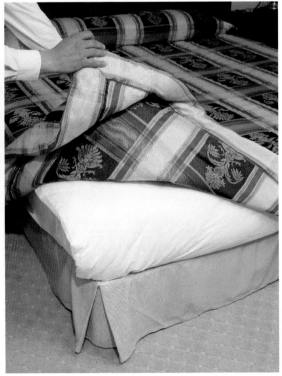

87/B

87/C

88/A   88/B

89/A

89/B

89/C

90/A

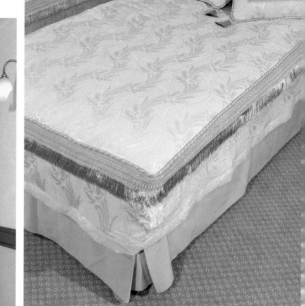

91/A

91/B

91/C

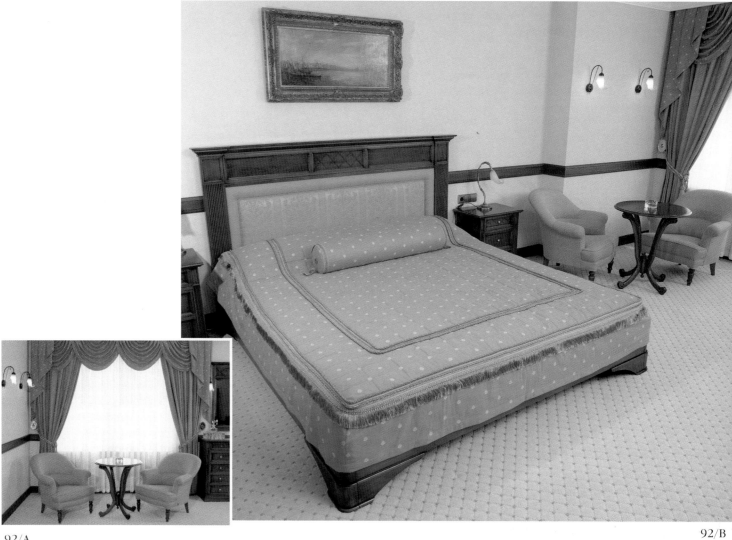

92/A

92/B

92/C

92/D

93/A

93/B

93/C

94/A

95/A

95/B

95/C

96/A

Valances

Whether pairing them with draperies, blinds, shutters or shades, whether in the bedroom, the study or the dining room, and whether decorating an extravagant bay window, a gothic arched window or a set of glazed French doors, valances are almost always a perfect fit. Perhaps the most diverse of window treatments, their capability to bring out the best in other window treatments is remarkable. In the bedroom, you may pair a pink tabbed valance with multi-colored draperies or a brilliant floral cloud valance with simple yellow curtains. In the living room, a soft ruffled valance will perfectly complement a set of wooden shutters or a balloon valance can be a subtle addition to a set of sheer curtains. And even when standing alone, valances will be a beautiful complement to your home.

Valances

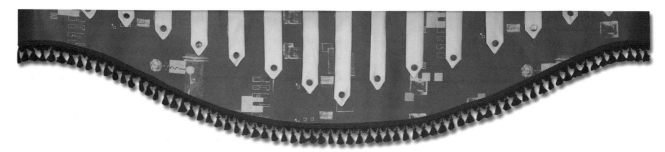

98/A

98/B

98/C

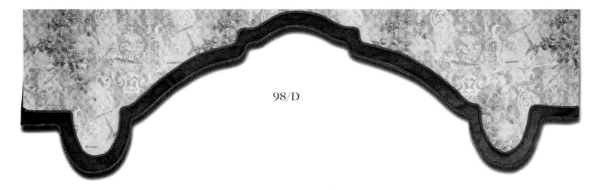

98/D

98/E

Valances

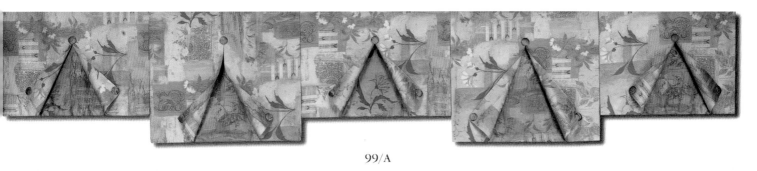

99/A

99/B

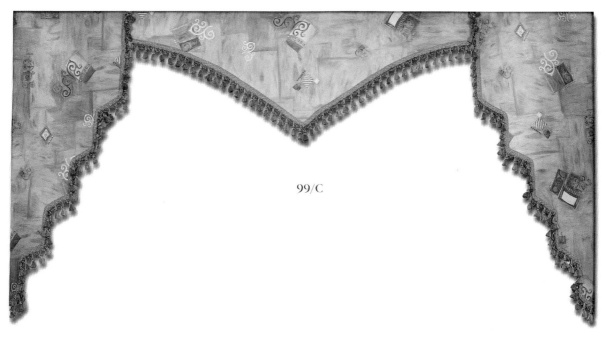

99/C

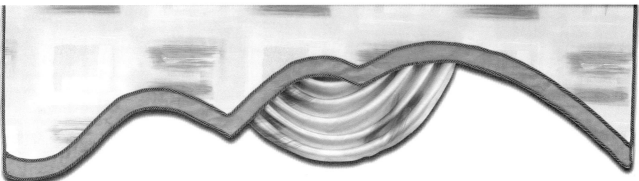

99/D

Valances

100/A

100/B

100/C

100/D

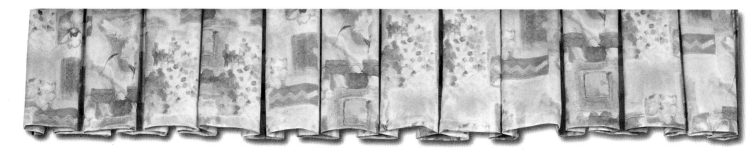

100/E

Valances

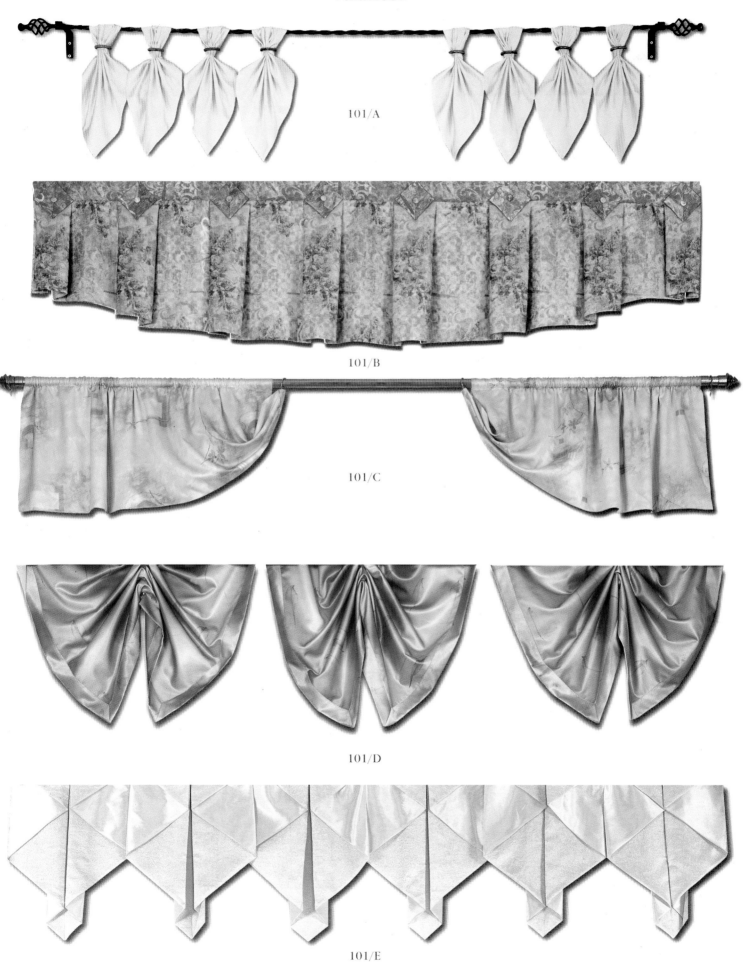

101/A

101/B

101/C

101/D

101/E

Valances

102/A

102/B

102/C

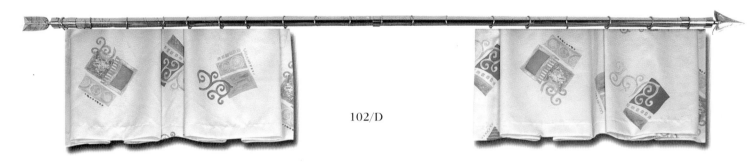

102/D

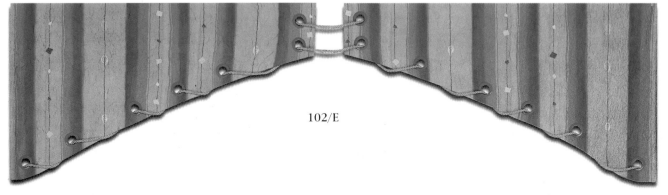

102/E

Home Fashions 102

Valances

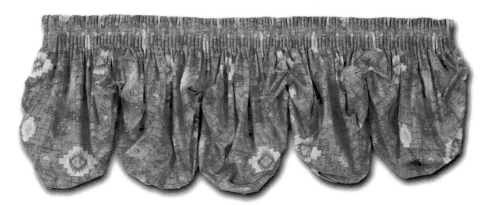

103/A

103/B

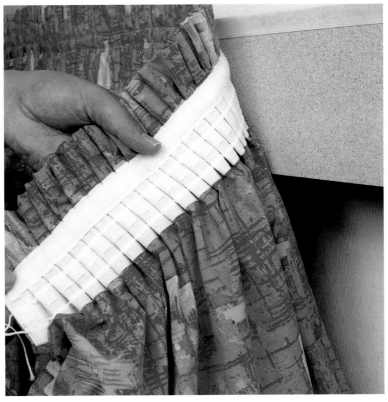

103/C

Valances

104/A

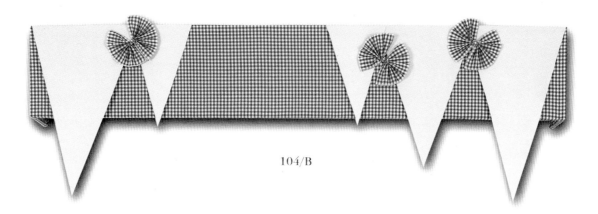

104/B

104/C

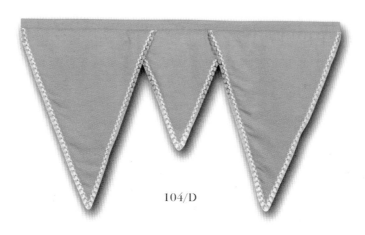

104/D

Valances

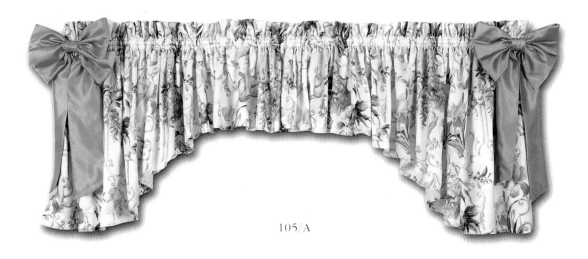

105/A

105/B

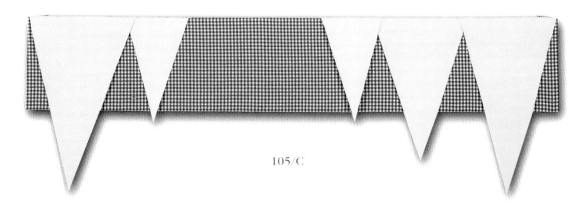

105/C

105/D

Valances

106/A

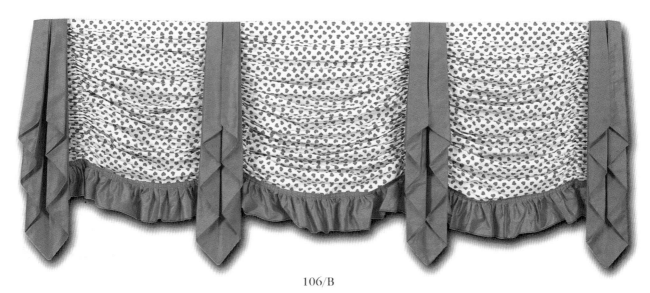

106/B

106/C

Valances

107/A

107/B

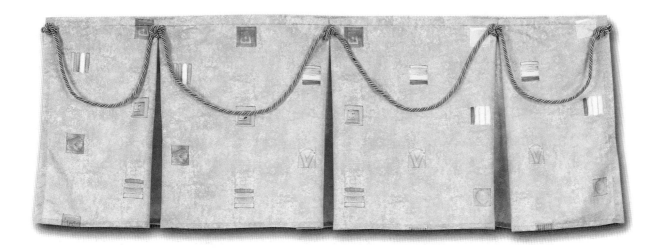

107/C

Valances

108/A

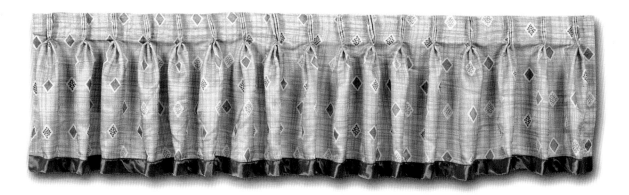

108/B

108/C

Valances

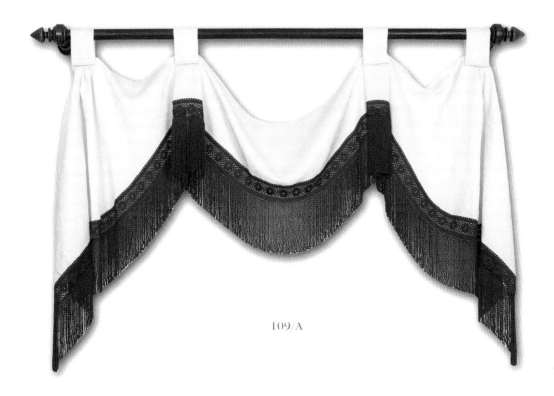

109/A

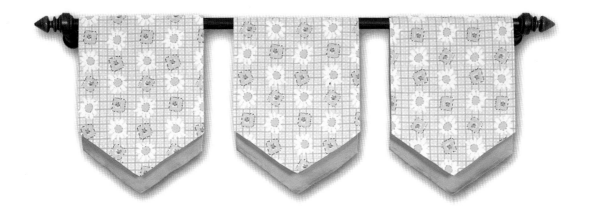

109/B

109/C

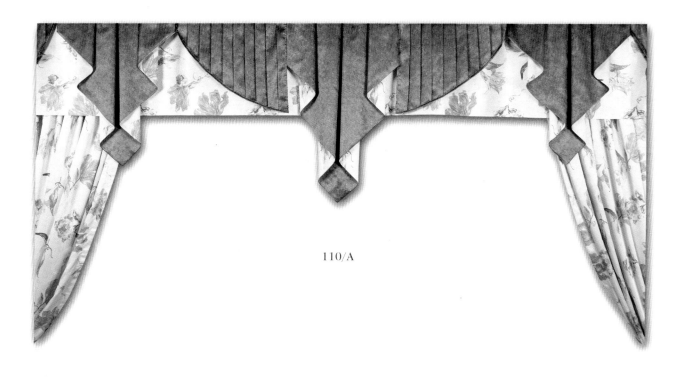

110/A

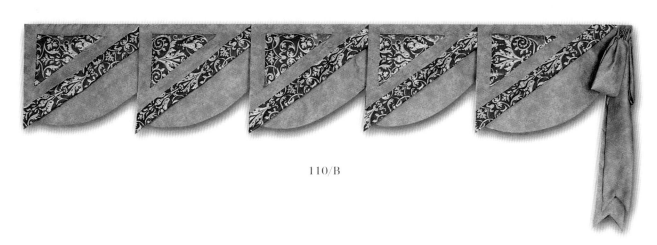

110/B

110/C

Valances

111/A

111/B

111/C

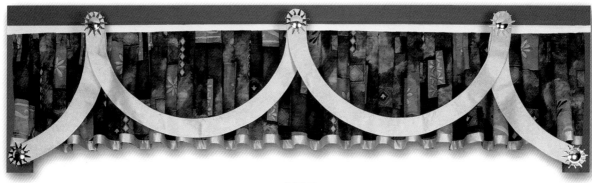

112/A

112/B

112/C

112/D

Valances

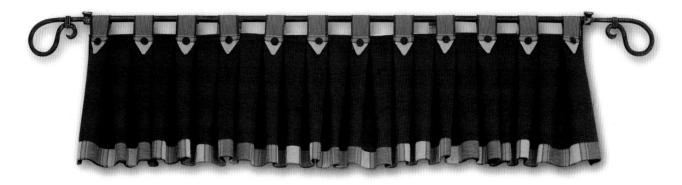

113/A

113/B

113/C

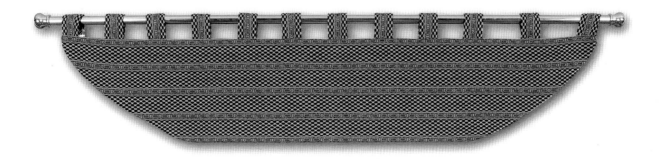

113/D

Valances

114/A

114/B

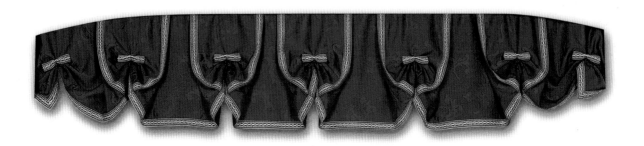

114/C

Valances

115/A

115/B

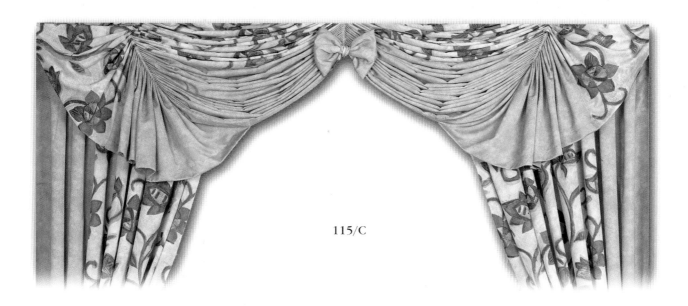

115/C

Valances

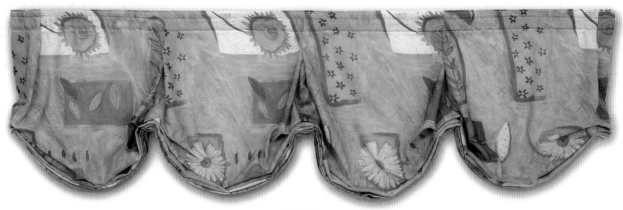

116/A

116/B

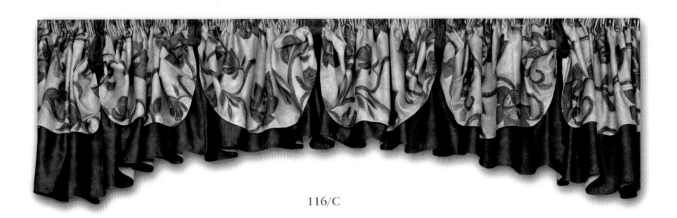

116/C

116/D

Home Fashions 116

Valances

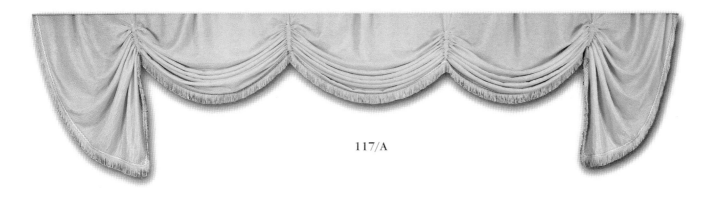

117/A

117/B

117/C

117/D

118/A

118/B

118/C

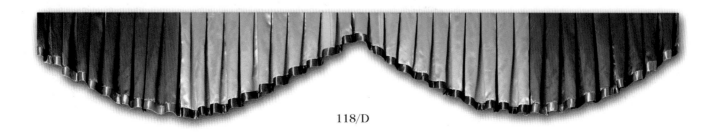

118/D

Valances

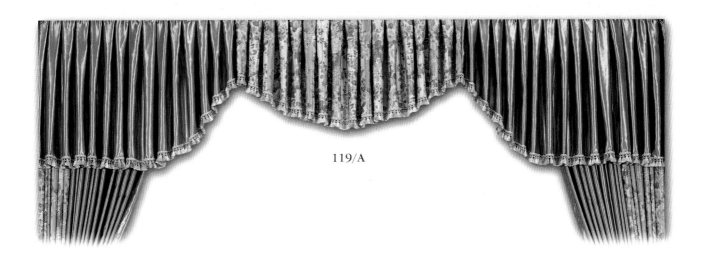

119/A

119/B

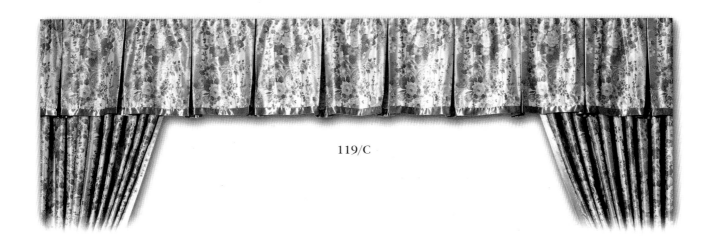

119/C

Valances

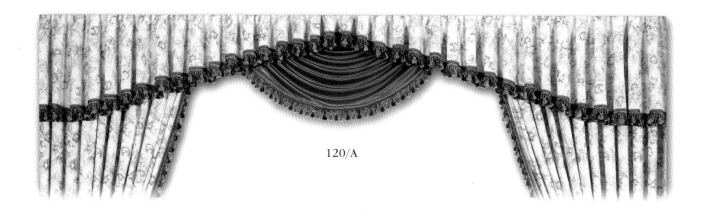

120/A

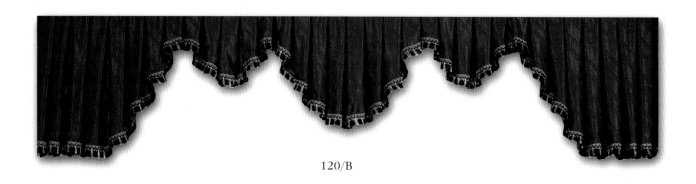

120/B

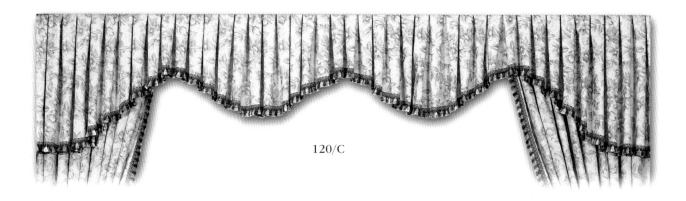

120/C

120/D

Valances

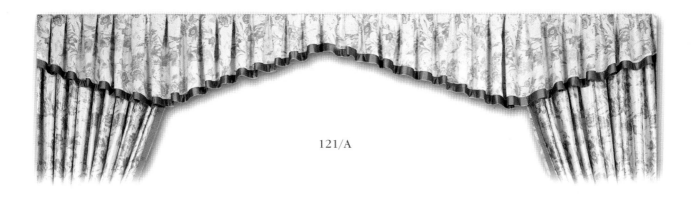

121/A

121/B

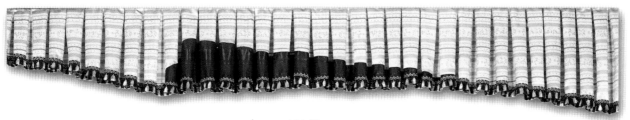

121/C

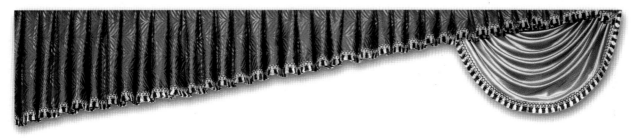

121/D

Valances

122/A

122/B

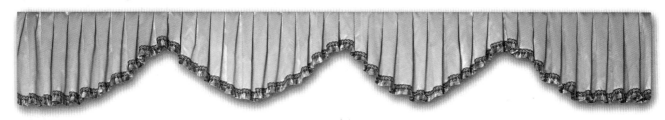

122/C

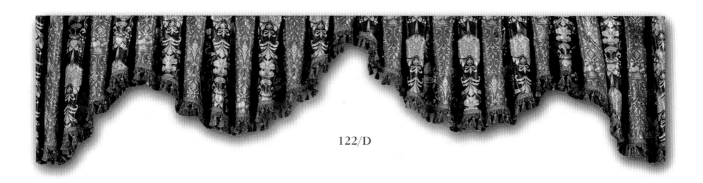

122/D

Valances

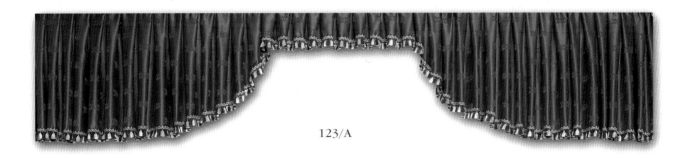

123/A

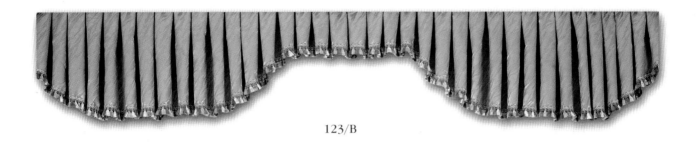

123/B

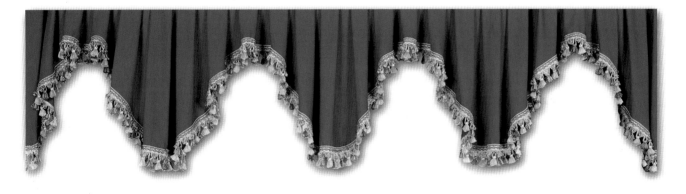

123/C

123/D

Valances

124/A

124/B

124/C

124/D

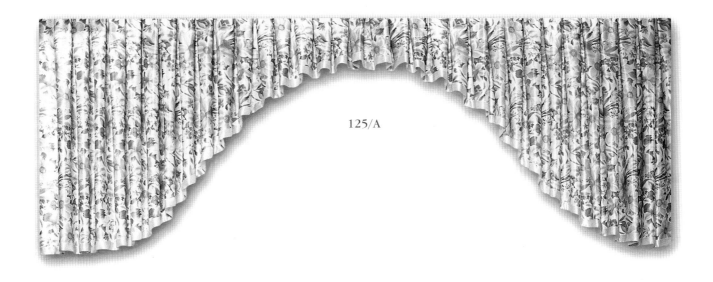

125/A

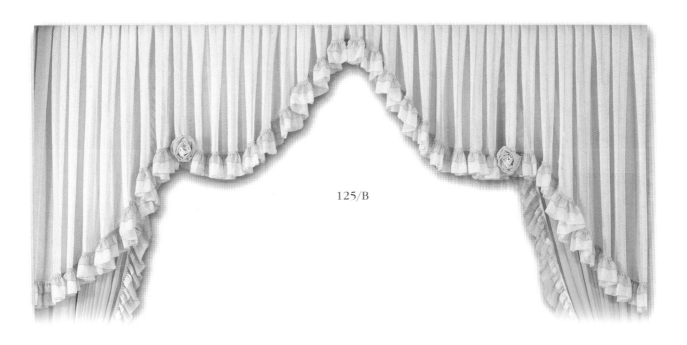

125/B

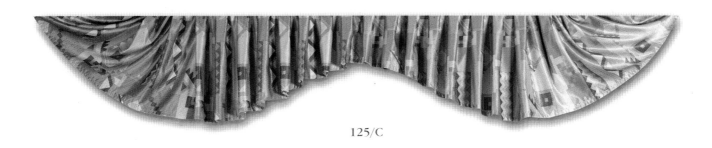

125/C

Valances

126/A

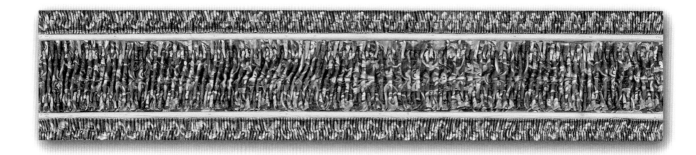

126/B

126/C

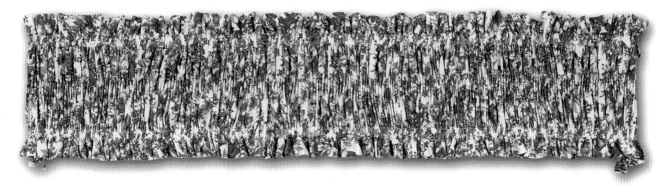

126/D

Swags and Cascades

Bring together a rich blue fabric, a classic iron rod and intricately detailed finials and a basic window can be transformed into a work of art. And with a swag and cascade combination, the possibilities are endless. Will the fabric surround the rod, covering it completely, or will you choose an open swag and expose the polished rod? Will the cascades be just slightly longer than the swags or will you allow the fabric to descend to the floor? Will the finials be simple or will you choose beautifully designed pieces that could stand alone in a museum hall? No matter how you decide to experiment with this window treatment, when creating a swag and cascade combination, you are limited only by your imagination.

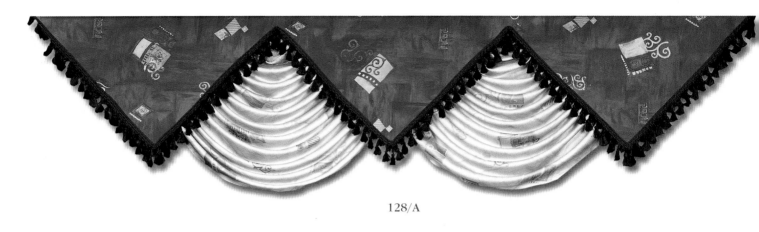

128/A

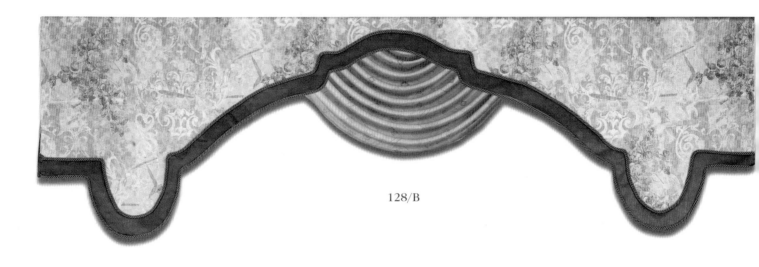

128/B

128/C

Swags and Cascades

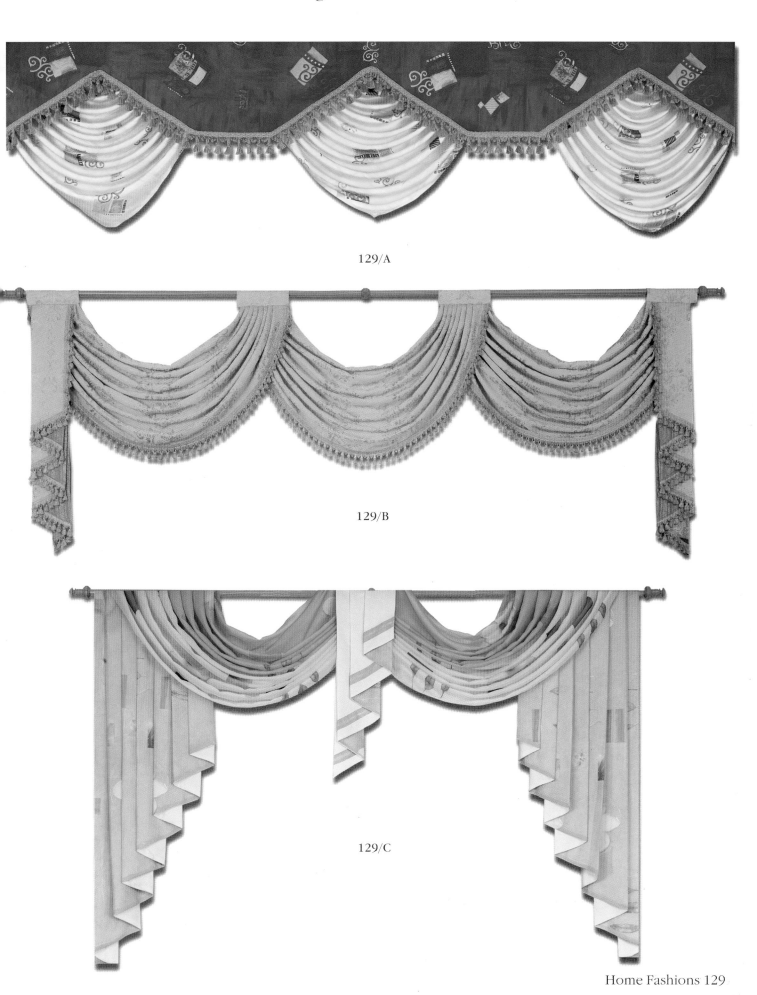

129/A

129/B

129/C

130/A

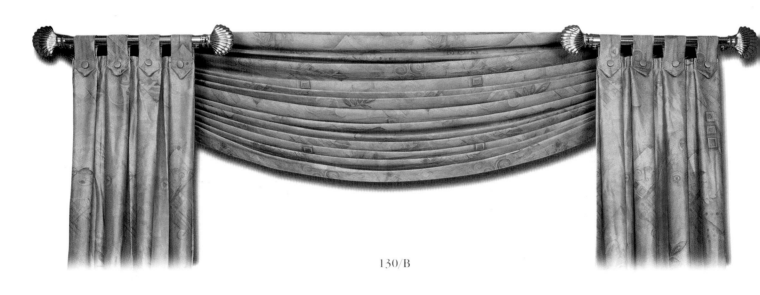

130/B

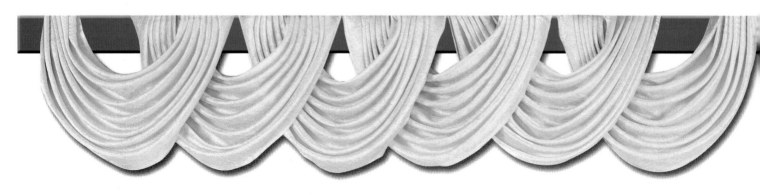

130/C

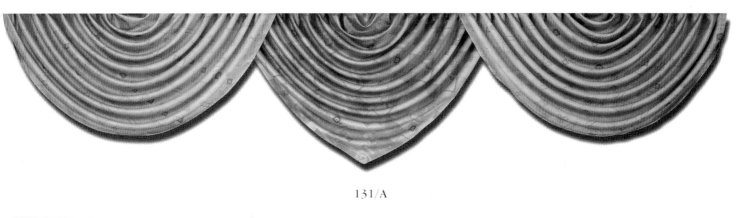

131/A

131/B

131/C

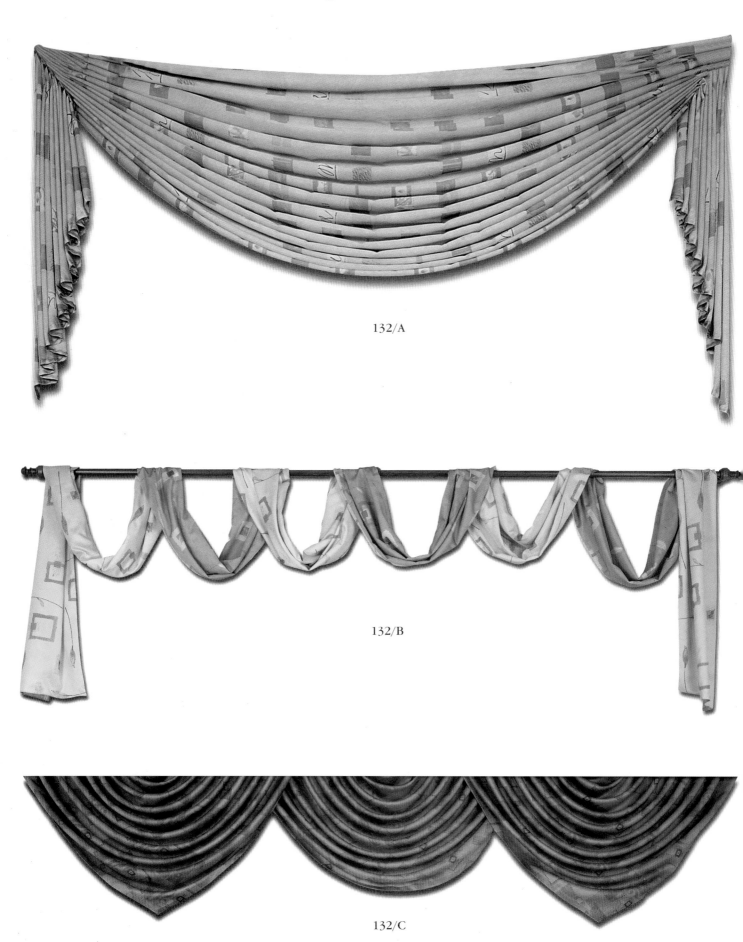

132/A

132/B

132/C

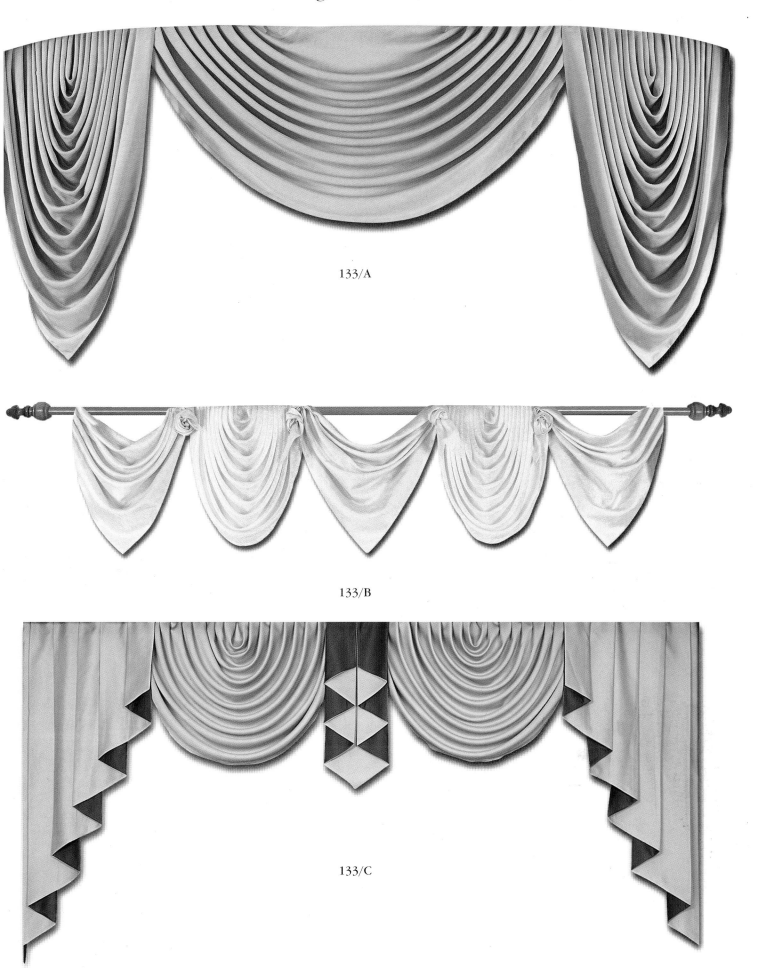

133/A

133/B

133/C

134/A

134/B

134/C

135/A

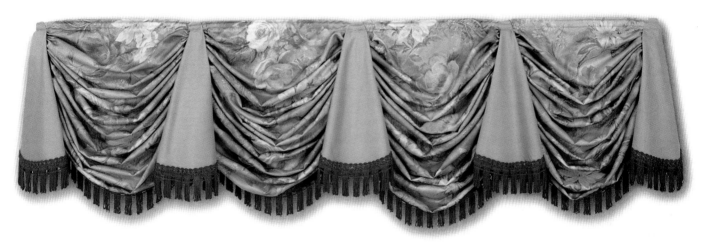

135/B

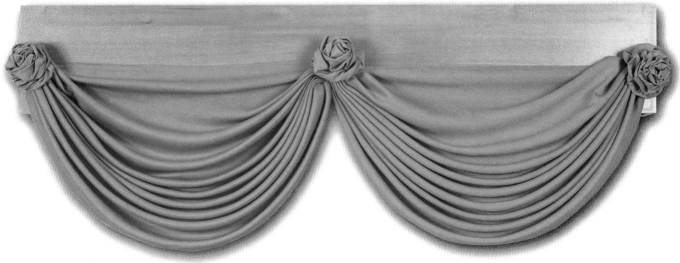

135/C

136/A

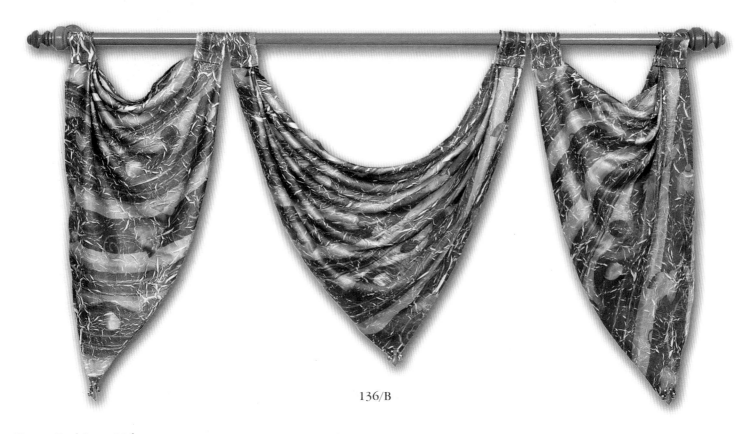

136/B

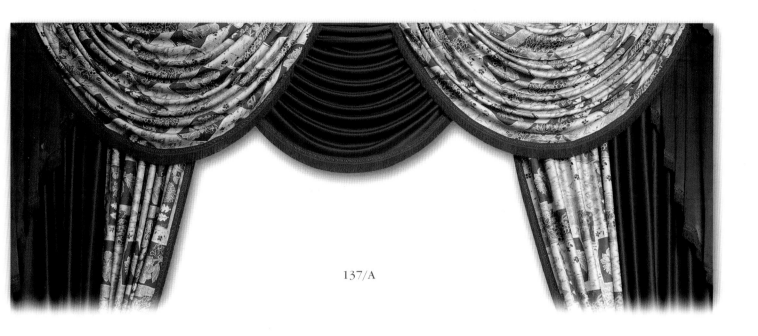

137/A

137/B

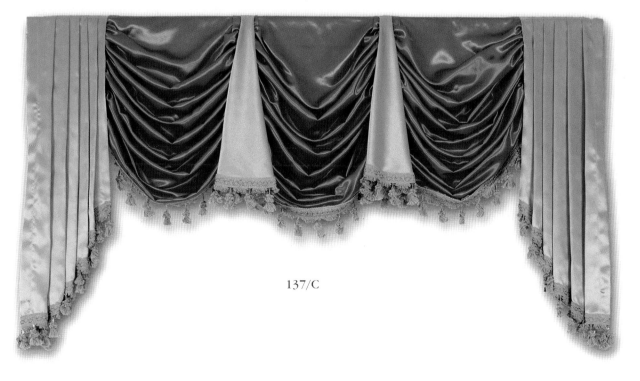

137/C

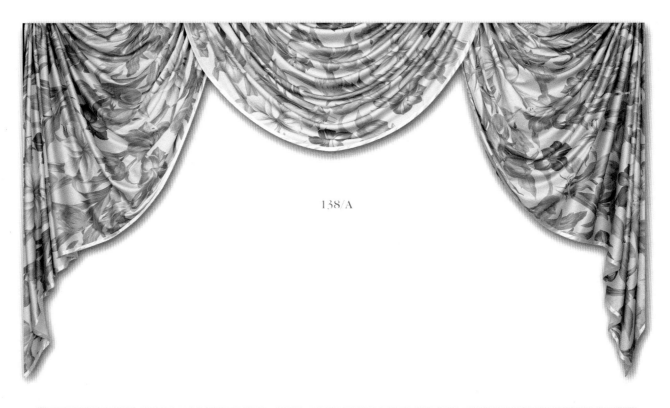

138/A

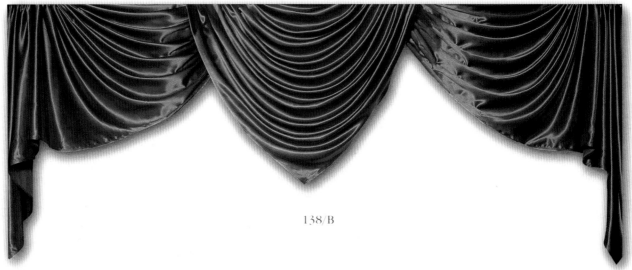

138/B

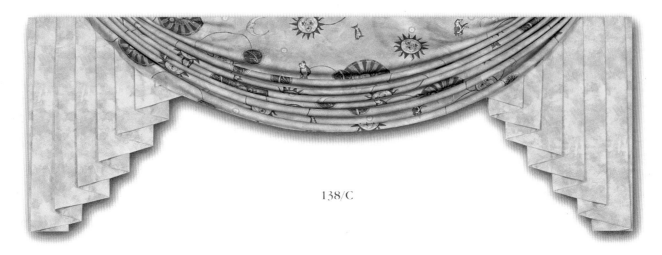

138/C

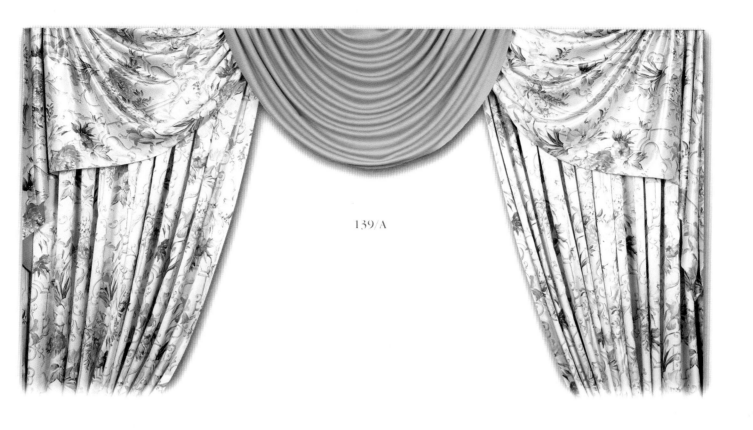

139/A

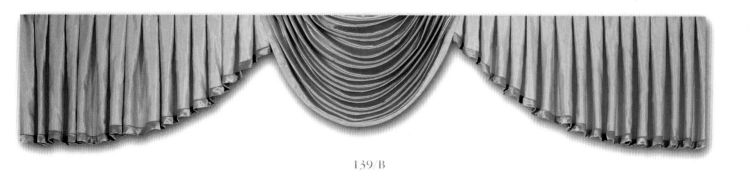

139/B

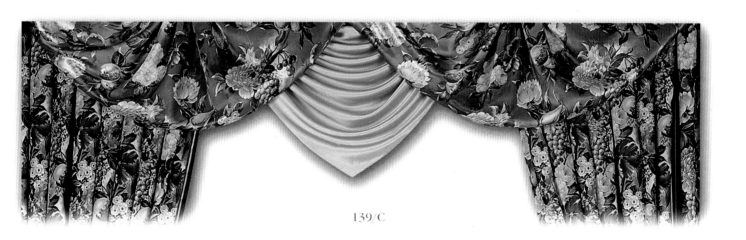

139/C

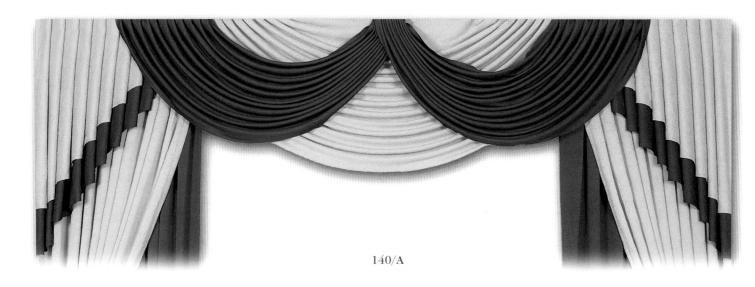

140/A

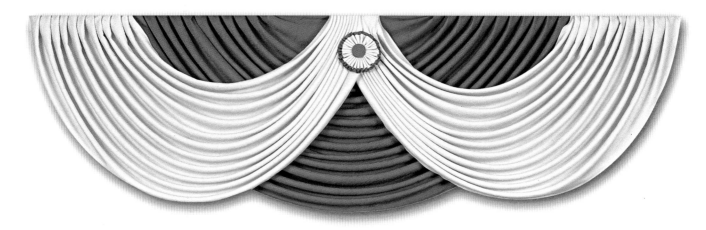

140/B

140/C

Swags and Cascades

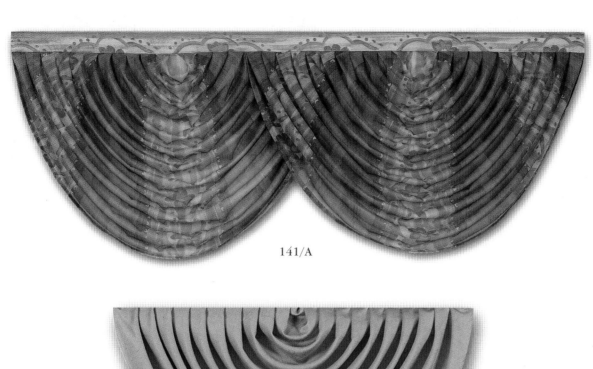

141/A

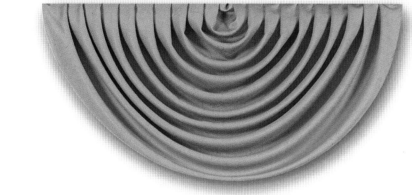

141/B

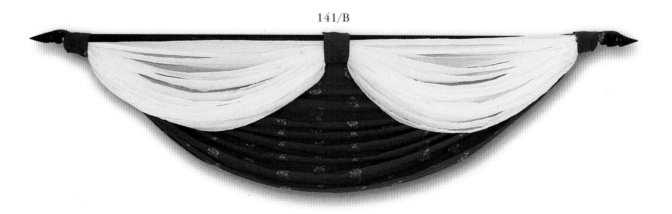

141/C

141/D

142/A

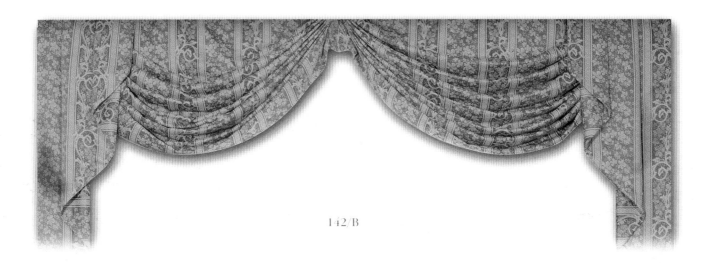

142/B

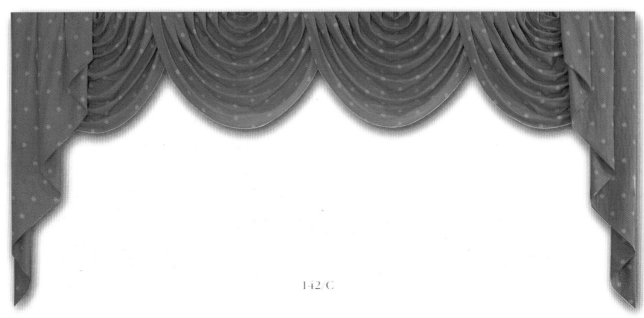

142/C

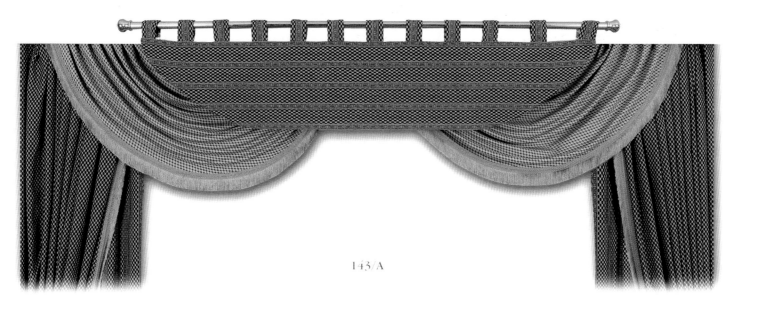

143/A

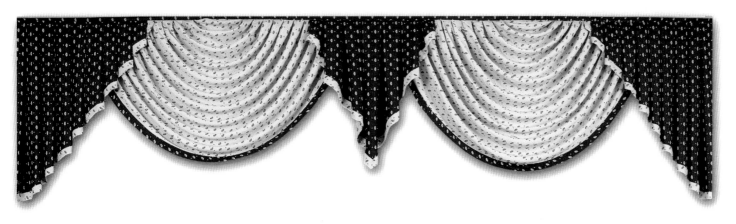

143/B

143/C

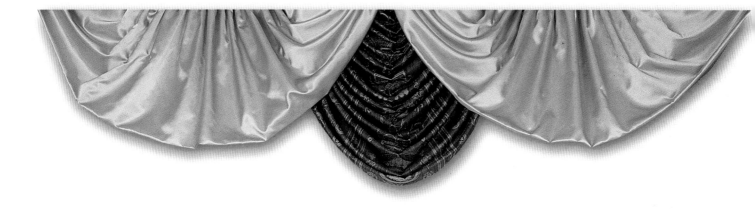

144/A

144/B

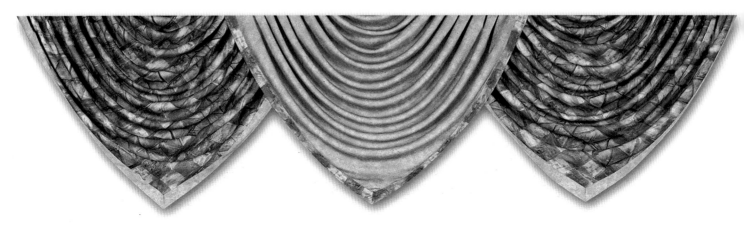

144/C

145/A

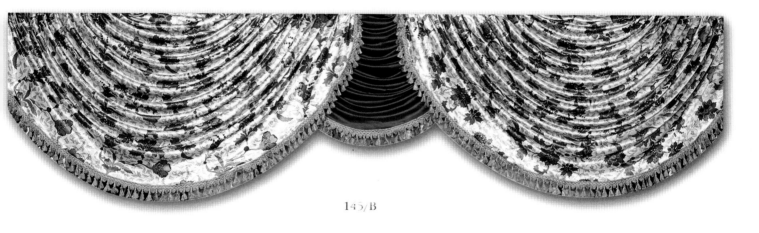

145/B

145/C

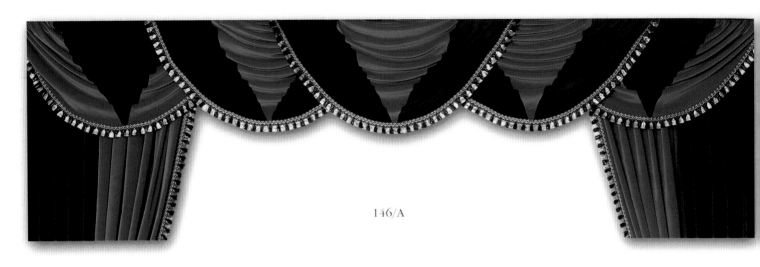

146/A

146/B

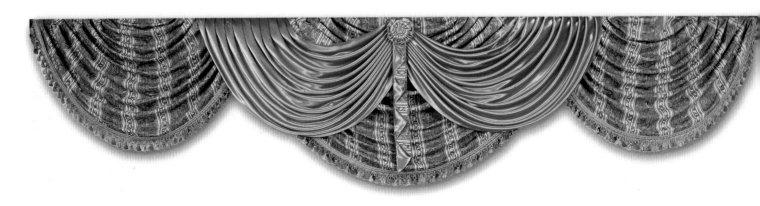

146/C

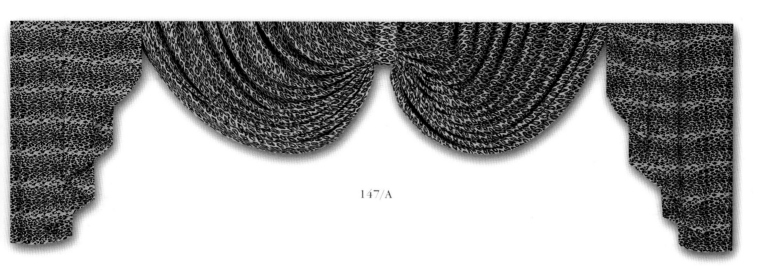

147/A

147/B

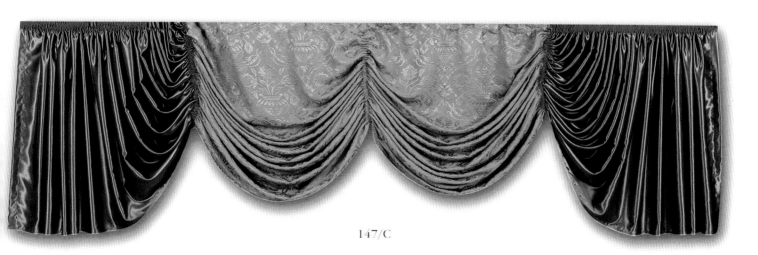

147/C

148/A

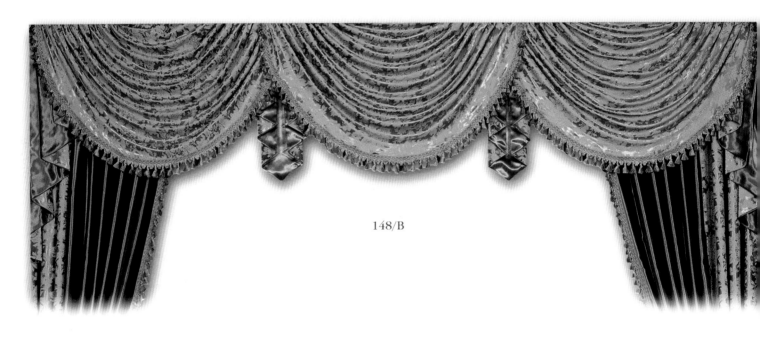

148/B

148/C

Swags and Cascades

149/A

149/B

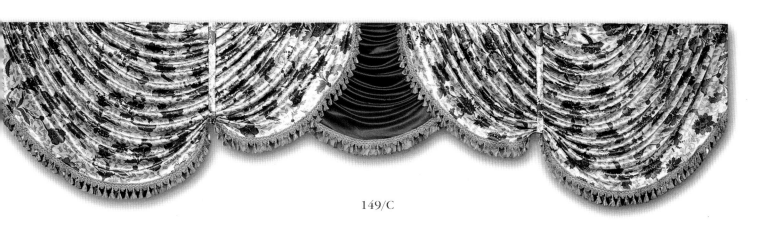

149/C

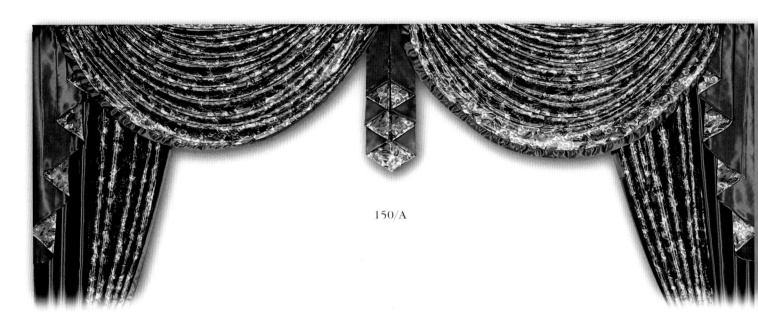

150/A

150/B

150/C

151/A

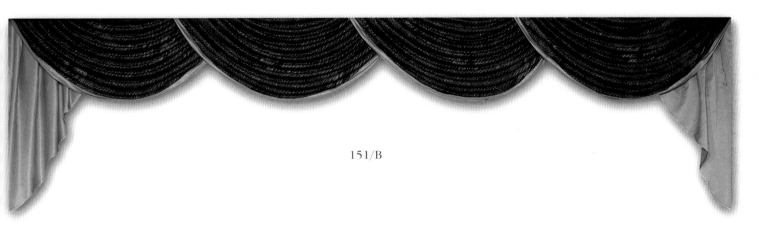

151/B

151/C

152/A

152/B

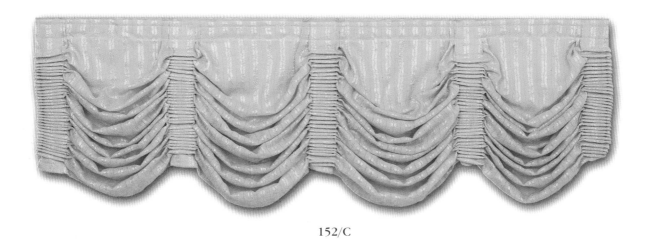

152/C

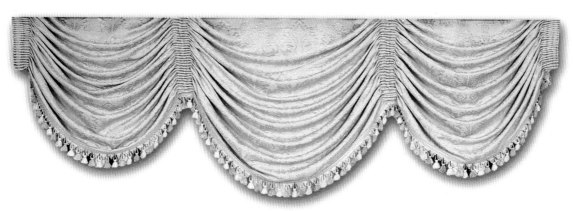

152/D

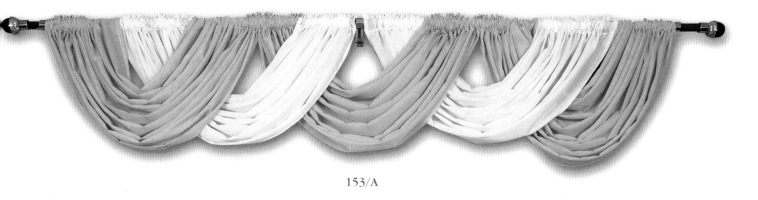

153/A

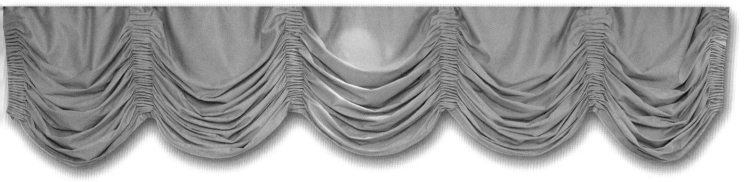

153/B

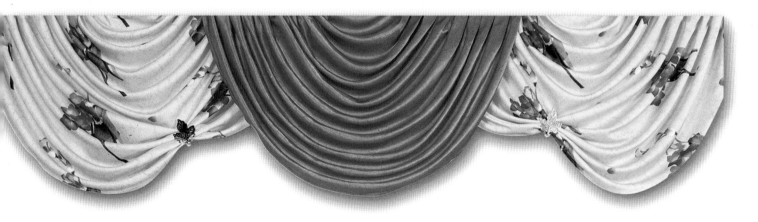

153/C

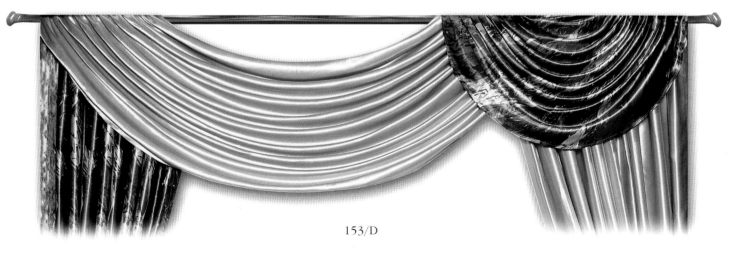

153/D

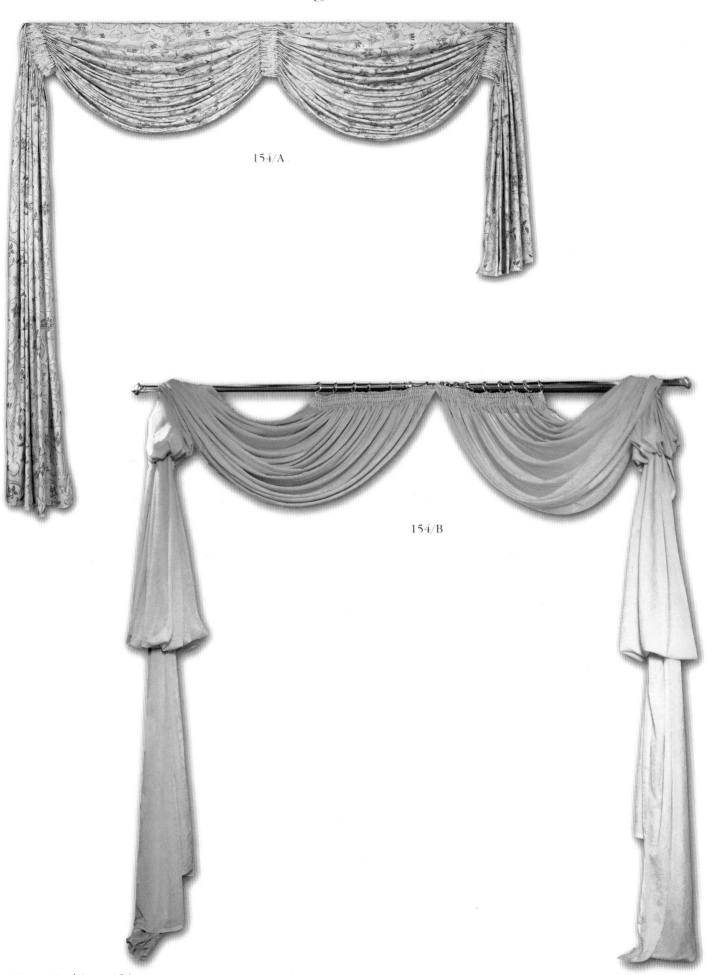

154/A

154/B

Kitchens and Bathrooms

It's a place to do homework or enjoy an afternoon snack. And despite a beautiful dining room, most dinner party guests somehow always end up there. It's the kitchen, and when decorating, it is a room that should not be forgotten.

Traditionally, a simple touch is all that is needed; such as pairing a light yellow roller shade with a matching balloon valance or perhaps a set of cream-colored vertical blinds and a blue cloud valance. Even without a practical accompaniment, a county-style tabbed valance will enhance the look of any kitchen window.

Another room where décor should not be forgotten is the bathroom.

For a classic bathroom, romantic sheer curtains are the perfect complement to an antique bathtub or for a dramatic look, a set of shower doors framed by tuxedo curtains can become the focal point of the room.

156/A

156/B

156/C

157/A

157/B

157/C

157/D

158/A

158/B

158/C

158/D

159/A

159/B

159/C

160/A

160/B

160/C

160/D

161/A

161/B

161/C

161/D

162/A

162/E

162/C

163/A

163/B

163/C

163/D

164/A

164/B

Tiebacks

With just a simple piece of braided rope or a measure of fabric, you can enjoy winter's first snowfall or a beautiful summer sunset without ever leaving the comfort of your home. In their most basic form, tiebacks will capture the fabric, gently holding the draperies to one side. And although they serve a functional purpose, tiebacks need not be a subtle addition to a window treatment. For a classic look, a tieback, made with fabric that perfectly matches the arched valance atop the window, can wrap itself around a set of pale blue curtains. For a dramatic touch, a tasseled tieback of red, green and gold can accompany draperies that hang from a brass rod. And for an unusual approach, a string of pearls can be used to tieback the pink curtains in the bedroom.

Tiebacks

166/A

166/B

166/C

166/D

Tiebacks

167/A

167/B

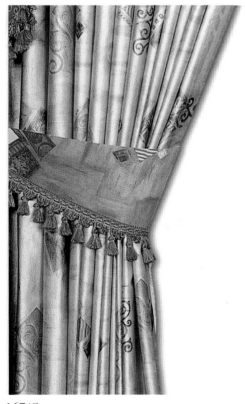

167/C

167/D

Tiebacks

168/A

168/B

168/C

168/D

Tiebacks

169/A

169/B

169/C

169/D

Tiebacks

170/A

170/B

170/C

170/D

Pillows and Accessories

Once the window treatments are complete and the furniture is in place, it is time to add those individual touches that make a house a home.

From pillows to lamps to tassels on the curtains, there are many things that make a room uniquely yours. A plain beige couch can be brought to life with brightly colored pillows or subtle flecks of gold can emerge from a Renaissance-style loveseat with the careful inclusion of a few deep yellow cushions. Will the room be decorated with lamps of all shapes and sizes or do you prefer a single lamp with the strength to fill the room? Does enough sunshine slip through the arched window or is a small lamp needed to enhance the natural light? And even the addition of a few decorated baskets can individualize any room in your home.

Pillows

172/A

172/D

172/B

172/E

172/C

172/F

Pillows

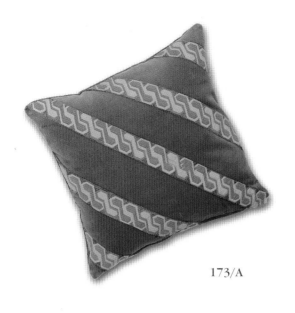

173/A

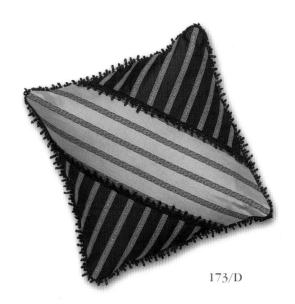

173/D

173/B

173/E

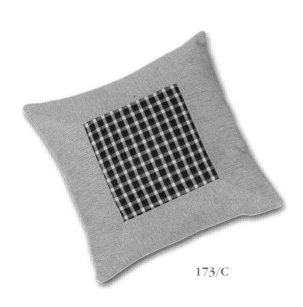

173/C

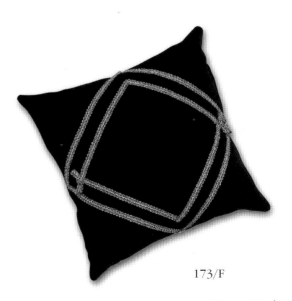

173/F

174/A

174/D

174/B

174/E

174/C

174/F

Pillows

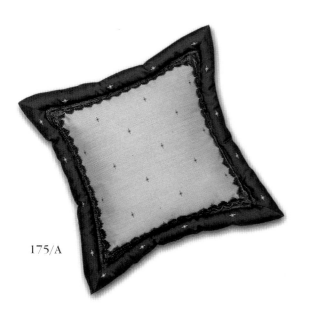

175/A

175/D

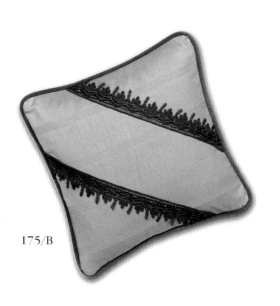

175/B

175/E

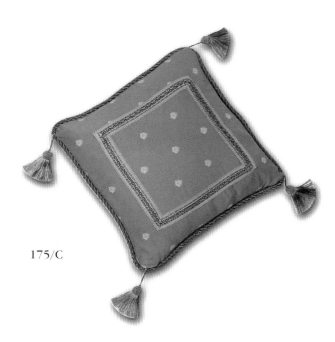

175/C

175/F

Pillows

176/A

176/D

176/B

176/E

176/C

176/F

Pillows

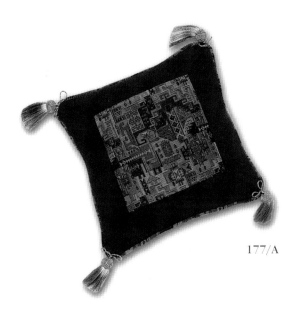

177/A

177/D

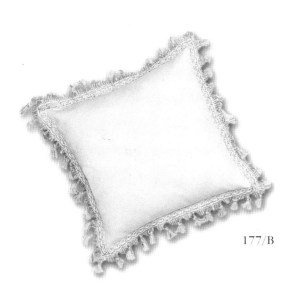

177/B

177/E

177/C

177/F

Pillows

178/A

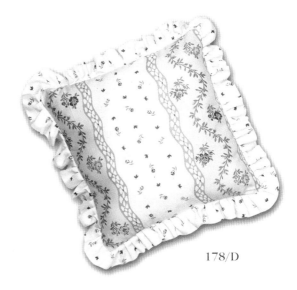

178/D

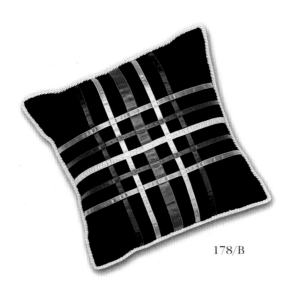

178/B

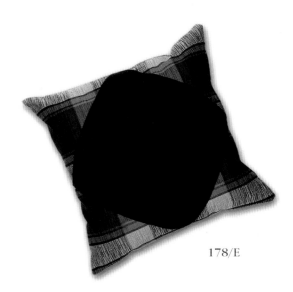

178/E

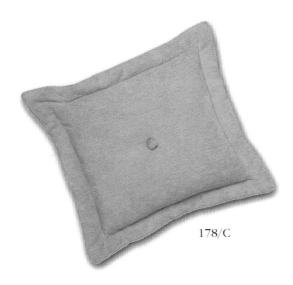

178/C

178/F

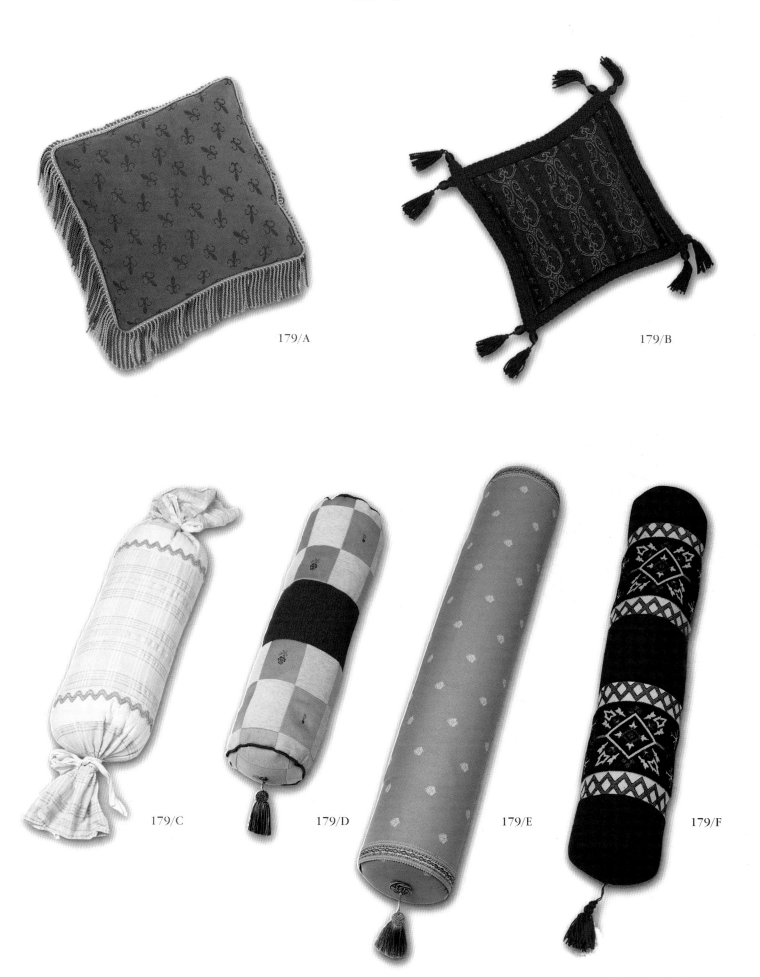

179/A

179/B

179/C

179/D

179/E

179/F

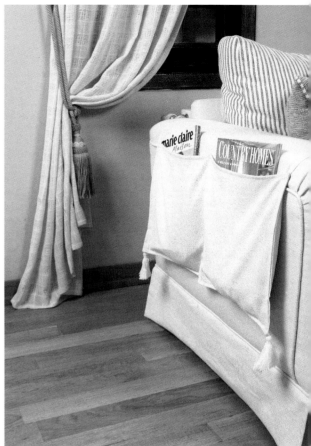

180/A

180/B

180/C

180/D

181/A

181/B

181/C

181/D

181/E

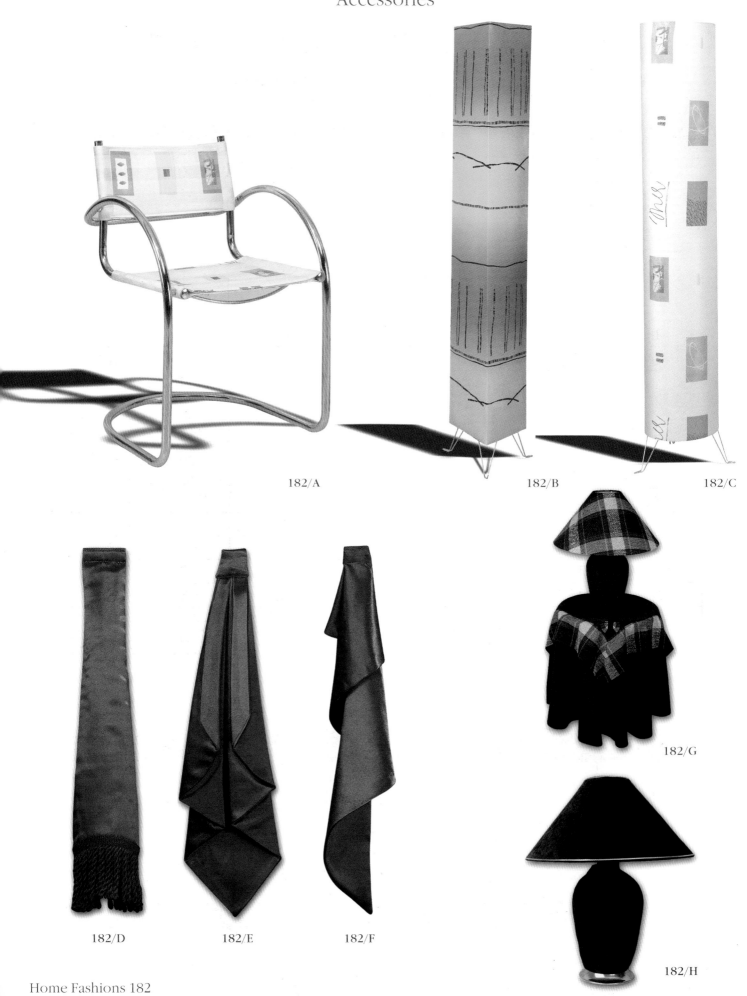

182/A

182/B

182/C

182/D

182/E

182/F

182/G

182/H

MEASUREMENT CONVERSION CHART

Inches to milimeters and cenimeters
mm - *milimeters* **cm** - *centimeters*

inches	mm	cm	inches	cm	inches	cm
1/8	3	0.3	9	22.9	30	76.2
1/4	6	0.6	10	25.4	31	78.7
3/8	10	1.0	11	27.9	32	81.3
1/2	13	1.3	12	30.5	33	83.8
5/8	16	1.6	13	33.0	34	86.4
3/4	19	1.9	14	35.6	35	88.9
7/8	22	2.2	15	38.1	36	91.4
1	25	2.5	16	40.6	37	94.0
1 1/4	32	3.2	17	43.2	38	96.5
1 1/2	38	3.8	18	45.7	39	99.1
1 3/4	44	4.4	19	48.3	40	101.6
2	51	5.1	20	50.8	41	104.1
2 1/2	64	6.4	21	53.3	42	106.7
3	76	7.6	22	55.9	43	109.2
3 1/2	89	8.9	23	58.4	44	111.8
4	102	10.2	24	61.0	45	114.3
4 1/2	114	11.4	25	63.5	46	116.8
5	127	12.7	26	66.0	47	119.4
6	152	15.2	27	68.6	48	121.9
7	178	17.8	28	71.1	49	124.5
8	203	20.3	29	73.7	50	127.0

yards	inches	meters	yards	inches	meters
1/8	4.5	0.11	1 1/8	40.5	1.03
1/4	9	0.23	1 1/4	45	1.14
3/8	13.5	0.34	1 3/8	49.5	1.26
1/2	18	0.46	1 1/2	54	1.37
5/8	22.5	0.57	1 5/8	58.5	1.49
3/4	27	0.69	1 3/4	63	1.60
7/8	31.5	0.80	1 7/8	67.5	1.71
1	36	0.91	2	72	1.83

Laundering Instructions

Regular/Normal Cycle with regular agitation and spin speed may be used.

Set dryer at any heat.

Iron - Ironing is needed.

Use Permanent Press/Wrinkle Resistant washer setting (which has a cool down or cold spray before the reduced spin).

Set dryer at High heat.

Iron using High temperature setting.

Use Gentle/Delicate washer setting (slow agitation and/or reduced wash time).

Set dryer at Medium heat.

Iron using Medium temperature setting.

Hand wash only.

Set dryer at Low heat.

Iron using Low temperature setting.

Do not wash.

No heat/air.

Do not iron or press with heat.

Machine dry.

Do not dry (used with do not wash).

Dryclean.

Use Normal Cycle setting.

Line dry/hang to dry - hang damp from line or bar and allow to dry.

Dryclean using any solvent.

Use Permanent Press/Wrinkle Resistant Cycle setting.

Drip dry - hang wet on plastic hanger and allow to dry with hand shaping only.

Dryclean using any solvent except trichloroethylene.

Use Gentle/Delicate Cycle setting.

Use only non-chlorine bleach (when needed).

Dryclean using Petroleum solvent only.

Do not tumble dry.

Do not bleach.

Do not dryclean.